Good Housekeeping
CHOCOLATE!
FAVORITE RECIPES FOR CAKES, COOKIES, PIES,
PUDDINGS & OTHER SUBLIME DESSERTS

Black-and-White Cupcakes (page 57)

Good Housekeeping

CHOCOLATE!

FAVORITE RECIPES FOR CAKES, COOKIES, PIES, PUDDINGS & OTHER SUBLIME DESSERTS

HEARST BOOKS
A division of Sterling Publishing Co., Inc.

New York / London
www.sterlingpublishing.com

GOOD HOUSEKEEPING

Rosemary Ellis
Editor in Chief

Sara Lyle
Lifestyle Editor

Susan Westmoreland
Food Director

Samantha B. Cassetty, M.S., R.D.
Nutrition Director

Sharon Franke
Food Appliances Director

BOOK DESIGN by Memo Productions
Photography Credits on page 174.

Library of Congress Cataloging-in-Publication Data is available.

10 9 8 7 6 5 4 3 2 1

The Good Housekeeping Cookbook Seal guarantees that the recipes in this cookbook meet the strict standards of the Good Housekeeping Research Institute. The Institute has been a source of reliable information and a consumer advocate since 1900, and established its seal of approval in 1909. Every recipe has been triple-tested for ease, reliability, and great taste.

Published by Hearst Books
A Division of Sterling Publishing Co., Inc.
387 Park Avenue South, New York, NY 10016

Good Housekeeping is a trademark of
Hearst Communications, Inc.

www.goodhousekeeping.com

For information about custom editions, special sales, premium and corporate purchases, please contact Sterling Special Sales Department at 800-805-5489 or specialsales@sterlingpublishing.com.

Distributed in Canada by Sterling Publishing
C/o Canadian Manda Group, 165 Dufferin Street
Toronto, Ontario, Canada M6K 3H6

Distributed in Australia by Capricorn Link
(Australia) Pty. Ltd.
P.O. Box 704, Windsor, NSW 2756 Australia

Manufactured in China

Sterling ISBN 978-1-58816-825-2

CONTENTS

FOREWORD 6

INTRODUCTION 8

1 CAKES & FROSTINGS | 16

2 PIES & TARTS | 76

3 COOKIES & CONFECTIONS | 102

4 MORE CHOCOLATY DESSERTS | 130

5 FINISHING TOUCHES | 158

INDEX 171

PHOTOGRAPHY CREDITS 174

METRIC EQUIVALENTS CHARTS 175

Silken Chocolate Cheesecake (page 61)

FOREWORD

Just talking about doing a chocolate cookbook raised the level of excitement in our test kitchens. As we looked at favorite chocolate recipes from the magazine and reminisced about every chocolate dessert we'd ever loved, it became clear that we were a group of—well—chocoholics.

We did have moments when all things chocolate were not sweet. When it came to the perfect chocolate layer cake, we disagreed, almost violently, on the proper frosting. The seven-minute fans in the crowd couldn't abide butter-cream, and the buttercream contingent couldn't imagine anything as insubstantial as "marshmallow" on rich chocolaty layers. We have taken the bipartisan approach and included both frostings as well as others, including my son's favorite, Peanut Butter Frosting.

Whether you are someone who keeps a stash of chocolate cookies in your desk to sate afternoon cravings or one who occasionally indulges in a Molten Chocolate Cake, *Chocolate!* has something to delight you. You'll find old favorites from the easiest One-Bowl Chocolate Cake to Classic Devil's Food Cake plus "company's coming" cakes including Chocolate Pound Cake with Irish Whiskey–Cream Sauce and Chocolate Génoise with Ganache. Lunchbox carriers will love Double Chocolate–Cherry Drops, Chocolate-Mint Sandwiches, and Apricot Fudgies. For a kids' get-together, try Whoopie Pies or Rich Chocolate Cupcakes with Malted-Milk Frosting. In addition to fabulous recipes, *Chocolate!* is filled with great tips to make your sweets look and taste wonderful. Each of these luscious recipes has been triple-tested in the Good Housekeeping Test Kitchens by our chocolate-loving staff, so they're guaranteed to be good.

SUSAN WESTMORELAND
Food Director, *Good Housekeeping*

Chocolate-Walnut Fudge (page 124), Double-Chocolate Biscotti (page 112) and more

INTRODUCTION

Chocolate, "Food of the Gods"

This book is for chocolate lovers who covet rich, fudge studded with crunchy walnuts; warm, fragrant chocolate cake with a melt-in-your-mouth molten center; or moist, mile-high devil's food layer cake filled with silky chocolate buttercream and festooned with chocolate curls. Our recipes are a collection of unabashedly rich, tempting, and sometimes downright decadent ways to enjoy chocolate, the "food of the gods." For many of us, a day without a chocolate treat is a day without sunshine; while for others, chocolate is a greatly anticipated and slowly savored occasional indulgence. Our intent is to deliver chocolate at its very best, whether in Old-Fashioned Cocoa Cake, Double-Chocolate Chunk Cookies, or Swiss Chocolate Almond Tart. We have included quick and easy recipes that can be prepared in mere minutes and others that are meant to fill a rainy afternoon. All of our recipes are written in the easy-to-follow, step-by-step *Good Housekeeping* style, so they will turn out perfect time after time, whether you are just learning your way around the kitchen or can cook with your eyes closed.

Chocolate: A Short History

Chocolate is commonly considered a modern-day sweet, but it has been around for several thousand years. Early on, the Mayas learned how to grow, harvest, ferment, roast, and grind cocoa seeds into a paste. The paste was mixed with water, chile peppers, and cornmeal and enjoyed as a bitter drink. By 1400, the Aztecs were trading with the Mayas for cocoa and used cocoa seeds and beans as currency. The Aztecs readily embraced the Mayas' bitter chocolate drink, but they considered it so special that it was reserved for rulers, priests, and decorated soldiers. The people of the court adored the drink, and it was common for as many as fifty portions of the *xocolatl* (pronounced shoco-latel) to be consumed in a day.

History was made in 1519, when Montezuma greeted the Spanish explorer Hernán Cortés with a goblet of the revered bitter chocolate brew. It didn't take long for Cortés to succumb to the drink's charms. He returned to Spain nine years later with cocoa seeds and the knowledge of how to turn them into the valuable paste. In Spain, the drink became all the rage at the court of King Charles V, where it was prepared with sugar and served hot.

By the mid-1600s, drinking chocolate had become a delightful habit in much of western Europe, as Italian and French visitors to Spain spread word of its charm. In London, an enterprising merchant opened the first of many chocolate houses, and before long, the Dutch were sending cocoa beans to America. In the 1700s, chocolate beverages were being sold as restoratives in Boston, and by 1765 James Baker had opened the first—and now oldest—chocolate company in America.

From this time forward, chocolate improved in leaps and bounds. The Austrians found that chocolate paste could be used to produce cakes. And in the 1800s, the Dutch figured out how to extract the cocoa butter from chocolate, thereby creating cocoa powder, which became a baking staple. In England, the availability of cocoa butter led to the creation of simple and delicious chocolate candy. Candy bars appeared in England by the mid 1800s, but it wasn't until nearly the end of the century that Rodolphe Lindt invented the process that resulted in the creamier, smoother chocolate that became known as Swiss chocolate.

Today's desserts and confections are a far cry from the first bitter chocolate drink that was enjoyed more than four hundred years ago. We live in a time when there are chocolates and chocolate desserts to suit every mood, every taste, and every occasion.

How Chocolate Is Made

In a way chocolate does grow on trees, the cacao tree, whose botanical name is *Theobroma cacao*, from the Greek for "food of the gods." Cacao trees need three things to thrive: high temperature, high humidity, and a special insect that pollinates its flowers. The flowers develop large pods that contain cocoa beans. The beans are removed from the pods and placed in piles to ferment, after which they are left in the sun to dry. The cocoa beans are then roasted and their papery husks removed by gently crushing the beans into little, irregular pieces known as nibs. The nibs are ground, and the fat they contain—cocoa butter—is then liquefied. The whole mixture is turned into a mass called chocolate liquor, which despite its name, is a solid and does not contain alcohol. The chocolate liquor is then used to make cocoa and chocolate for all the world to enjoy.

Types of Chocolate

Unsweetened chocolate is simply ground cocoa beans. Professionals call it chocolate liquor. It is harsh and bitter tasting and is never eaten out of hand. It is most often used in baking in combination with semi-sweet chocolate.

Bittersweet chocolate has been sweetened, but the amount of sugar varies from brand to brand. Some bittersweet chocolates list the percentage of chocolate liquor: a chocolate with 70 percent is more bitter and has a more intense flavor than one with 64 percent.

Semisweet chocolate is similar to bittersweet chocolate, although it is usually a bit sweeter. It can be used interchangeably with bittersweet chocolate in most recipes. It is available in 1-ounce squares, in small bars, and in bulk at specialty food stores.

German's sweet chocolate, used to make German chocolate cake, is sold under a brand name and should not be confused with bittersweet or semisweet chocolate.

Milk chocolate contains dried milk powder and a high percentage of sugar. It is essentially an eating chocolate—it's not usually used for baking.

White chocolate is not really chocolate at all but is rather vanilla-flavored sweetened cocoa butter (a by-product of chocolate processing), although some mid-priced brands substitute vegetable fat for the cocoa butter.

Unsweetened cocoa is what provides the rich chocolate flavor in many desserts. There are two kinds of cocoa powder: natural and Dutch-process. In baking, they are not interchangeable. Natural cocoa has a full, rich flavor and is the type most commonly used in American kitchens. It is nearly always used in combination with baking soda. Dutch-process cocoa is treated with an alkalai that reduces its acidity. It gives baked goods a rich, dark color, and it doesn't need to be combined with baking soda. For a hot cup of cocoa, use your favorite.

Chocolate Basics

Storing Chocolate Chocolate is best stored in a cool, dry place, such as a pantry. Or wrap the chocolate in an airtight heavy plastic bag and place in the crisper drawer of your refrigerator. To prevent the chocolate from developing condensation, let it come to room temperature while still wrapped before chopping or breaking it up. If chocolate is stored at warmer temperatures, it may develop a "bloom" (caused by the cocoa butter rising to the surface), or grayish streaks on the outside. This is just a cosmetic problem. Chocolate with a bloom is perfectly fine to melt and use in cooking or baking.

Chopping Chocolate Use a large chef's knife or heavy serrated knife to cut chocolate into pieces. Be sure the cutting board is perfectly clean and dry. To finely chop chocolate, cut it into small pieces (about ¼ inch) by hand, then pulse it in a food processor fitted with the metal blade until finely chopped.

Melting Chocolate There is a simple rule when it comes to melting chocolate: Keep the heat low and the chocolate dry. Even one tiny drop of water can cause the chocolate to "seize up" (stiffen), which ruins it. There are two easy ways to melt chocolate, in the microwave or in a double boiler or bowl set over simmering water. It is not a good idea to melt chocolate in a saucepan unless it has been combined with other ingredients such as cream or butter and the saucepan is heavy.

Before melting chocolate, always chop or break it into little pieces (about ¼ inch) so it can melt quickly and evenly. To melt chocolate on the stovetop, place it in a bowl on top of a double boiler set over—not in—a pan containing about 1½ inches of simmering water on low heat. Stir occasionally with a heat-safe spatula until the chocolate is melted and smooth, then set the bowl on the counter. To melt chocolate in a microwave, place the chopped chocolate in a microwave-safe bowl. Heat it on Low or Medium-Low power at 30-second intervals, stirring after each interval, to see if the chocolate has melted. When chocolate is heated in the microwave, it continues to hold its shape even when melted.

Kitchen Basics

You do not have to be an experienced cook to turn out fabulous chocolate desserts. The key to success is threefold: Use the right ingredients, measure them accurately, and use the proper equipment. Keep this in mind and you are guaranteed to turn out perfect chocolate desserts time after time. Be sure to read a recipe in its entirety to familiarize yourself with it before you begin. Make sure you have all the necessary ingredients on hand. And do not substitute ingredients or baking pans unless the recipe indicates that you may do so.

INGREDIENT KNOW-HOW

Butter vs. Margarine Many of our recipes offer the option of using either butter or margarine. Butter is usually listed first as it will give you the most delicious flavor and texture. If you do use margarine, make sure it contains 80 percent fat. Do not substitute light margarine or vegetable-oil spreads. Do not use whipped butter. Soften butter or margarine by letting it stand, still wrapped, at room temperature for about 30 minutes or just until pliable—not soft or melty. Cutting it into small pieces will speed up the process.

Flour We use all-purpose or cake flour in most of our recipes—they are not interchangeable. All-purpose flour is a blend of hard and soft wheats. Cake flour is made from soft wheat, so it produces cakes with an especially delicate texture. Do not use self-rising flour; it already has salt and a leavener added.

Baking Powder and Baking Soda Baking powder is a blend of baking soda, cream of tartar, and cornstarch. Store it tightly closed in a cool, dry place. It's a good idea to replace it every six months. Baking soda, also known as bicarbonate of soda, is used when a recipe contains an acid ingredient, such as buttermilk, molasses, yogurt, chocolate, or sour cream. Dutch-process cocoa does not have to be combined with baking soda, as Dutching reduces its acidity.

Eggs Our recipes call for "large" grade eggs. We do not recommend substituting a different size. Store eggs in their original container in the refrigerator.

Sugar Granulated white sugar is our baking basic. Superfine sugar dissolves very quickly, making it excellent for meringues. Confectioners' sugar (also called powdered sugar) is very finely ground and contains cornstarch. It is a good idea to sift it before use, as it can be lumpy. Brown sugar (light and dark) is granulated sugar with some molasses added. Dark brown and light brown sugar are interchangeable in most of our recipes.

Extracts It takes just a few drops of these concentrated flavorings to perfume a cake or a batch of cookies or confections. Use pure—not imitation—extracts whenever possible. Vanilla is the extract most used in desserts. Try a few different brands and see which you prefer—they do vary. Other extracts to keep on hand are almond, orange, lemon, and peppermint.

MEASURING KNOW-HOW

If you measure ingredients correctly, you will have consistent baking results. In your kitchen you need liquid measuring cups (at least 1- and 2-cup sizes), a set of nesting metal dry measuring cups, and a set of measuring spoons. Butter does not need to be measured, as each stick is premarked with all of the measurements you will need.

Liquids We recommend clear glass measuring cups. To measure a liquid accurately, place the cup on the counter and add the desired amount of liquid. Bend down to check the accuracy of the measure at eye level (do not lift up the cup). Tip: Before measuring sticky ingredients such as corn syrup or honey, coat the inside of the liquid measuring cup with cooking spray and they will slide out easily.

Dry Ingredients To measure flour or sugar, first stir the ingredient with a fork or whisk to aerate it, as it tends to get packed down. Lightly spoon flour into the metal measuring cup to overflowing, then level it off with a narrow metal spatula or the straight edge of a knife. To measure brown sugar or vegetable shortening, pack it firmly into the cup, then level it off.

EQUIPMENT KNOW-HOW

Time was, a sturdy bowl, a wooden spoon, and a rolling pin were all you needed to turn out sweet treats. These days there seem to be almost limitless possibilities when it comes to baking equipment and tools, but the truth is, you need only the following items to get most jobs done well.

Electric mixer A hand mixer is sufficient, but if you have a sturdy stand mixer, by all means use it.

Cake Pans Three 8- and 9-inch round pans.

Metal Baking Pans 8- and 9-inch square pans and a 13" by 9" pan.

Glass or Ceramic Baking Dishes Have several on hand, including 13" by 9", 10" by 15", and 11" by 7".

Other Useful Pans 10- and 12-cup Bundt pans, 9" by 3" and 10" by 2¼" springform pans, 9- and 10-inch tube pans, 9- and 11-inch removable-bottom tart pans, 9" by 5" and 8½" by 4½" loaf pans, 15" by 10" jelly-roll pans.

Basic Tools Mixing bowls, large heavy cookie sheets, wire cooling racks, regular and mini muffin pans, custard cups, heat-safe rubber spatula, wire whisk, parchment paper, pastry bags and tips, rolling pin, instant-read thermometer, pastry brush.

Baked Chocolate-Hazelnut Puddings (page 140)

CAKES & FROSTINGS

Baking cakes is a precise process that requires the correct ingredients, accurate measuring, and directions that must be followed to a tee. Cake batter should be made with room-temperature ingredients. Remove butter, eggs, and dairy products from the refrigerator about 30 minutes ahead. Soften butter until it is malleable—not shiny and melting. Room-temperature eggs can be beaten to their greatest volume.

Most of our recipes call for all purpose flour, but occasionally cake flour is used. If you don't have cake flour, here's an easy substitution: For every cup of flour, spoon 2 tablespoons cornstarch into a 1-cup measure. Spoon in enough bleached all-purpose flour to fill the cup, then level it off.

PAN PREP To line a pan, place it on a piece of waxed paper. Use a pencil to trace around the bottom of the pan, then cut out the round. To grease the pan, apply an even layer of vegetable shortening using a folded piece of paper towel. To flour the pan, sprinkle about 1 table-spoon of flour into the greased pan, then tilt it to coat the bottom and side; tap out the excess.

OVEN SMARTS Position the racks before turning on the oven, and pre-heat thoroughly. Always use an oven thermometer. When baking a single cake or two layers, place them in the center of the oven. If baking more layers, stagger them in the upper and lower thirds of the oven. Cakes baked in tube pans should be placed in the lower third of the oven.

STORAGE Refrigerate cakes that contain fillings or frostings made of dairy products. Unfrosted butter cakes can be stored at room tempera-ture for about three days. Foam cakes dry out quickly; store them at room temperature for up to two days.

Chocolate Layer Cake (page 18)

CHOCOLATE LAYER CAKE

Nothing says "celebration" like frosted chocolate layers—which may be the reason this cake has reappeared countless times in *Good Housekeeping* since 1927. (For photo, see page 16).

ACTIVE TIME: 35 MINUTES · **TOTAL TIME:** 1 HOUR PLUS COOLING
MAKES: 16 SERVINGS

2	CUPS ALL-PURPOSE FLOUR	1	CUP GRANULATED SUGAR
1	CUP UNSWEETENED COCOA	3	LARGE EGGS
1½	TEASPOONS BAKING SODA	2	TEASPOONS VANILLA EXTRACT
¼	TEASPOON SALT	1½	CUP LOW-FAT BUTTERMILK
¾	CUP BUTTER OR MARGARINE (1½ STICKS), SOFTENED		INTENSE CHOCOLATE BUTTER FROSTING (PAGE 64)
1	CUP PACKED BROWN SUGAR		

1 Preheat oven to 350°F. Grease three 8-inch round cake pans. Line bottoms with waxed paper; grease paper. Dust pans with flour (page 45).

2 On another sheet of waxed paper, combine flour, cocoa, baking soda, and salt. In large bowl, with mixer at low speed, beat butter and brown and granulated sugars until blended. Increase speed to high; beat 5 minutes or until pale and fluffy, occasionally scraping bowl with rubber spatula.

3 Reduce speed to medium-low; add eggs one at a time, beating well after each addition. Beat in vanilla until blended. Add flour mixture alternately with buttermilk, beginning and ending with flour mixture; beat just until batter is smooth, occasionally scraping bowl with rubber spatula.

4 Spoon batter evenly among prepared pans. Place two pans on upper oven rack and one on lower rack so pans are not directly above one another. Bake 22 to 25 minutes or until toothpick inserted in center of cake comes out clean. Cool layers in pans on wire racks 10 minutes. Run thin knife around layers to loosen from sides of pans. Invert onto wire racks then remove and discard waxed paper; cool completely.

5 Meanwhile, prepare Intense Chocolate Butter Frosting. Place one cake layer, rounded side down, on cake plate; spread ⅓ cup frosting over layer. Top with second layer, rounded side down; spread ⅓ cup frosting over layer. Place remaining layer, rounded side up, on top. Spread remaining frosting over side and top of cake.

EACH SERVING: ABOUT 495 CALORIES | 7G PROTEIN | 55G CARBOHYDRATE | 30G TOTAL FAT (18G SATURATED) | 4G FIBER | 98MG CHOLESTEROL | 415MG SODIUM

ONE-BOWL CHOCOLATE CAKE

One-bowl recipes are lifesavers when you need to bake a party-pretty layer cake in record time. The only trick is to be sure to have the butter soft enough to blend easily into the batter.

ACTIVE TIME: 20 MINUTES · **TOTAL TIME:** 50 MINUTES PLUS COOLING

MAKES: 12 SERVINGS

2   CUPS ALL-PURPOSE FLOUR

1   CUP GRANULATED SUGAR

¾   CUP PACKED BROWN SUGAR

⅔   CUP UNSWEETENED COCOA

1½ TEASPOONS BAKING POWDER

½   TEASPOON BAKING SODA

½   TEASPOON SALT

1½ CUPS MILK

½   CUP BUTTER OR MARGARINE (1 STICK), SOFTENED

2   LARGE EGGS

2   TEASPOONS VANILLA EXTRACT

PEANUT BUTTER FROSTING (PAGE 71)

1   Preheat oven to 350°F. Grease two 9-inch round cake pans.

2   In large bowl, combine flour, granulated and brown sugars, cocoa, baking powder, baking soda, salt, milk, butter, eggs, and vanilla. With mixer at low speed, beat until dry ingredients are moistened. Increase speed to high; beat until batter is smooth, about 3 minutes.

3   Divide batter equally between prepared pans. Bake cake until toothpick inserted in center comes out clean, about 30 minutes. Cool layers in pans on wire racks 10 minutes. Run thin knife around layers to loosen from sides of pans. Invert onto racks to cool completely.

4   Meanwhile, prepare Peanut Butter Frosting. Place one cake layer, rounded side down, on cake plate. With narrow metal spatula, spread ½ cup frosting over layer. Top with second layer, rounded side up. Spread remaining frosting over side and top of cake.

EACH SERVING: ABOUT 550 CALORIES | 9G PROTEIN | 72G CARBOHYDRATE | 27G TOTAL FAT (13G SATURATED) | 3G FIBER | 90MG CHOLESTEROL | 470MG SODIUM

EASY CHOCOLATE-BUTTERMILK CAKE

This cake is so delectably moist and chocolaty, it can be served without any frosting at all.

ACTIVE TIME: 30 MINUTES · **TOTAL TIME:** 1 HOUR PLUS COOLING
MAKES: 16 SERVINGS

2¼ CUPS ALL-PURPOSE FLOUR

¾ CUP UNSWEETENED COCOA

1¾ CUPS SUGAR

2 TEASPOONS BAKING SODA

1¼ TEASPOONS SALT

1½ CUPS BUTTERMILK

1 CUP VEGETABLE OIL

3 LARGE EGGS

1½ TEASPOONS VANILLA EXTRACT

WHITE CHOCOLATE BUTTERCREAM FROSTING (PAGE 68)

1 Preheat oven to 350°F. Grease two 9-inch round cake pans or one 10-inch Bundt pan. Dust with cocoa (page 45).
2 In large bowl, combine flour, cocoa, sugar, baking soda, and salt.
3 In medium bowl, with wire whisk, mix buttermilk, oil, eggs, and vanilla until blended. Add buttermilk mixture to flour mixture; whisk until smooth.
4 Divide batter equally between prepared round pans or pour all into Bundt pan; spread evenly. Bake until toothpick inserted in center comes out clean, about 30 minutes for 9-inch layers, or about 40 minutes for Bundt cake. Cool in pans on wire racks 10 minutes. Run thin knife around layers to loosen from sides of pan. Or, if using Bundt pan, run tip of knife around edge of cake to loosen. Invert onto racks to cool completely.
5 Meanwhile, prepare White Chocolate Buttercream Frosting. For layer cake, place one layer, rounded side down, on cake plate. With narrow metal spatula, spread ⅔ cup frosting over layer. Top with second layer, rounded side up. Spread remaining frosting over side and top of cake. For Bundt, either frost with buttercream or serve plain.

EACH SERVING: ABOUT 525 CALORIES | 5G PROTEIN | 61G CARBOHYDRATE | 31G TOTAL FAT (12G SATURATED) | 2G FIBER | 72MG CHOLESTEROL | 505MG SODIUM

OLD-FASHIONED COCOA CAKE

Mayonnaise is the secret ingredient in this moist sheet cake, which is finished with a thick layer of chocolate buttercream. A great bring-along for a casual party.

ACTIVE TIME: 30 MINUTES · **TOTAL TIME:** 1 HOUR 5 MINUTES PLUS COOLING
MAKES: 18 SERVINGS

2½ CUPS ALL-PURPOSE FLOUR

1½ CUPS SUGAR

¾ CUP UNSWEETENED COCOA

1½ TEASPOONS BAKING SODA

¾ TEASPOON SALT

1½ CUPS BUTTERMILK

¾ CUP MAYONNAISE

1 TABLESPOON VANILLA EXTRACT

2 LARGE EGGS

RICH CHOCOLATE FROSTING (PAGE 62)

1 Preheat oven to 350°F. Grease 13" by 9" baking pan.

2 In large bowl, combine flour, sugar, cocoa, baking soda, and salt.

3 In medium bowl, with wire whisk, mix buttermilk, mayonnaise, vanilla, and eggs until almost smooth.

4 With wooden spoon, stir buttermilk mixture into flour mixture until smooth. Spoon into prepared baking pan. Bake until toothpick inserted in center comes out clean, 35 to 40 minutes. Cool cake in pan on wire rack.

5 Meanwhile, prepare Rich Chocolate Frosting. With narrow metal spatula, spread frosting over cake.

EACH SERVING: ABOUT 385 CALORIES | 5G PROTEIN | 52G CARBOHYDRATE | 20G TOTAL FAT (4G SATURATED) | 2G FIBER | 28MG CHOLESTEROL | 380MG SODIUM

RICH CHOCOLATE CAKE

An extra-generous amount of unsweetened cocoa makes this cake the most chocolaty ever. We like it slathered with Fluffy White Frosting, but you can use any frosting you like.

ACTIVE TIME: 45 MINUTES · **TOTAL TIME:** 1 HOUR 25 MINUTES PLUS COOLING
MAKES: 20 SERVINGS

2	CUPS ALL-PURPOSE FLOUR	2	CUPS SUGAR
1	CUP UNSWEETENED COCOA	4	LARGE EGGS
2	TEASPOONS BAKING POWDER	2	TEASPOONS VANILLA EXTRACT
1	TEASPOON BAKING SODA	1⅓	CUPS MILK
½	TEASPOON SALT		FLUFFY WHITE FROSTING (PAGE 72)
1	CUP BUTTER OR MARGARINE (2 STICKS), SOFTENED		

1 Preheat oven to 350°F. Grease 13" by 9" baking pan. Line bottom with waxed paper; grease paper. Dust pan with flour (page 45).

2 In bowl, combine flour, cocoa, baking powder, baking soda, and salt.

3 In large bowl, with mixer at low speed, beat butter and sugar until blended. Increase speed to high; beat until light and fluffy, about 5 minutes. Reduce speed to medium-low; add eggs, one at a time, beating well after each addition. Beat in vanilla. Mixture may appear grainy. Reduce speed to low; add flour mixture alternately with milk, beginning and ending with flour mixture. Beat until batter is smooth, occasionally scraping bowl with rubber spatula.

4 Pour batter into prepared pan. Bake until toothpick inserted in center comes out almost clean, 40 to 45 minutes. Cool in pan on wire rack 10 minutes. Run thin knife around cake to loosen from sides of pan. Invert onto rack. Remove waxed paper; cool completely.

5 Meanwhile, prepare Fluffy White Frosting. With narrow metal spatula, spread frosting over cake.

EACH SERVING: ABOUT 285 CALORIES | 4G PROTEIN | 43G CARBOHYDRATE | 12G TOTAL FAT (7G SATURATED) | 2G FIBER | 70MG CHOLESTEROL | 291MG SODIUM

CLASSIC DEVIL'S FOOD CAKE

Devil's food cake is a twentieth-century creation. No one knows for sure how the cake got its name, but many believe it was due to its dark color and richness—it is the opposite of light and delicate angel food cake.

ACTIVE TIME: 35 MINUTES · **TOTAL TIME:** 1 HOUR 5 MINUTES PLUS COOLING
MAKES: 16 SERVINGS

---

2 CUPS ALL-PURPOSE FLOUR	1 CUP GRANULATED SUGAR
1 CUP UNSWEETENED COCOA	3 LARGE EGGS
1½ TEASPOONS BAKING SODA	1½ TEASPOONS VANILLA EXTRACT
½ TEASPOON SALT	1½ CUPS BUTTERMILK
½ CUP BUTTER OR MARGARINE (1 STICK), SOFTENED	RICH CHOCOLATE FROSTING (PAGE 62)
1 CUP PACKED LIGHT BROWN SUGAR	

1 Preheat oven to 350°F. Grease three 8-inch round cake pans. Line bottoms with waxed paper; grease paper. Dust pans with flour (page 45).

2 In medium bowl, combine flour, cocoa, baking soda, and salt.

3 In large bowl, with mixer at low speed, beat butter and brown and granulated sugars until blended. Increase speed to high; beat until light and fluffy, about 5 minutes. Reduce speed to medium-low; add eggs, one at a time, beating well after each addition. Beat in vanilla. Add flour mixture alternately with buttermilk, beginning and ending with flour mixture; beat just until batter is smooth, occasionally scraping bowl with rubber spatula.

4 Divide batter equally among prepared pans; spread evenly. Place two pans on upper oven rack and one pan on lower oven rack so pans are not directly above one another. Bake until toothpick inserted in center comes out clean, 30 to 35 minutes. Cool layers in pans on wire rack 10 minutes. Run thin knife around layers to loosen from sides of pans. Invert onto racks. Remove waxed paper; cool completely.

5 Meanwhile, prepare Rich Chocolate Frosting. Place one cake layer, rounded side down, on cake plate. With narrow metal spatula, spread ⅓ cup frosting over layer. Top with second layer, rounded side up, and spread ⅓ cup frosting over layer. Place remaining layer, rounded side up, on top. Spread remaining frosting over side and top of cake.

EACH SERVING: ABOUT 450 CALORIES | 5G PROTEIN | 74G CARBOHYDRATE | 17G TOTAL FAT (10G SATURATED) | 3G FIBER | 72MG CHOLESTEROL | 355MG SODIUM

GERMAN'S CHOCOLATE CAKE

Contrary to what most people think, this beloved chocolate cake is not a German creation. The correct name is German's, which was the brand name of an American baking chocolate from which it was first created.

ACTIVE TIME: 45 MINUTES · **TOTAL TIME:** 1 HOUR 15 MINUTES PLUS COOLING
MAKES: 16 SERVINGS

2	CUPS ALL-PURPOSE FLOUR	1½	CUPS SUGAR
1	TEASPOON BAKING SODA	¾	CUP BUTTER OR MARGARINE (1½ STICKS), SOFTENED
¼	TEASPOON SALT		
1¼	CUPS BUTTERMILK	4	SQUARES (4 OUNCES) SWEET BAKING CHOCOLATE, MELTED
1	TEASPOON VANILLA EXTRACT		COCONUT-PECAN FROSTING (PAGE 70)
3	LARGE EGGS, SEPARATED		

1 Preheat oven to 350°F. Grease three 8-inch round cake pans. Line bottoms with waxed paper; grease paper. Dust pans with flour (page 45).
2 In small bowl, combine flour, baking soda, and salt. In measuring cup, mix buttermilk and vanilla.
3 In medium bowl, with mixer at medium-high speed, beat egg whites until frothy (page 53). Sprinkle in ¾ cup sugar, 1 tablespoon at a time, beating until soft peaks form when beaters are lifted.
4 In large bowl, with mixer at medium speed, beat butter until light and fluffy. Add remaining ¾ cup sugar and beat until well blended. Reduce speed to medium-low; add egg yolks, one at a time, beating well after each addition. Beat in melted chocolate. Reduce speed to low; add flour mixture alternately with buttermilk mixture, beginning and ending with flour mixture. Beat until smooth, occasionally scraping bowl. With rubber spatula, fold half of beaten egg whites into batter; gently fold in remaining egg whites.
5 Divide batter equally among prepared pans. Place two pans on upper oven rack and one pan on lower oven rack so pans are not directly above one another. Bake until toothpick inserted in center comes out almost clean, about 30 minutes. Cool in pans on wire racks 10 minutes. Run thin knife around layers to loosen from sides of pans. Invert onto racks. Remove waxed paper; cool completely.

FROSTING LAYER CAKES

It is easiest to frost a cake if it is elevated and can be turned. If you don't have a cake decorating stand, place the cake on a serving plate set on a large coffee can or inverted bowl.

Brush off any crumbs and use a serrated knife to trim away any crisp edges. Place the first layer, rounded side down, on the serving plate. To keep the plate clean, tuck strips of waxed paper under the cake, covering the plate edge. Using a narrow metal spatula, spread ½ to ⅔ cup frosting on the cake layer top, spreading it almost to the edge. Top with the second cake layer, rounded side up. Thinly frost the cake to set the crumbs and keep them in place; first coat the top of the cake, then the side. Finish the cake with a thicker layer of frosting. Where the top and side of the frosting meet, smooth it by sweeping and swirling the edge of the frosting toward the center of the cake. Slip out the waxed paper strips and discard.

6 Meanwhile, prepare Coconut-Pecan Frosting. Place one layer, rounded side down, on cake plate. With narrow metal spatula, spread 1 cup frosting over layer. Top with second cake layer, rounded side up, and spread with 1 cup frosting. Place remaining layer, rounded side up, on top. Spread remaining frosting over side and top of cake.

EACH SERVING: ABOUT 505 CALORIES | 5G PROTEIN | 53G CARBOHYDRATE | 31G TOTAL FAT (16G SATURATED) | 2G FIBER | 140MG CHOLESTEROL | 320MG SODIUM

CHECKERBOARD CAKE

This cake is the best of both worlds: vanilla cake and chocolate cake rolled into one. Special checkerboard cake pans are available, but our easy, clever method uses standard round cake pans.

ACTIVE TIME: 40 MINUTES · **TOTAL TIME:** 1 HOUR 5 MINUTES PLUS COOLING
MAKES: 16 SERVINGS

3½ CUPS CAKE FLOUR (NOT SELF-RISING)

1 TABLESPOON BAKING POWDER

½ TEASPOON SALT

1 CUP BUTTER OR MARGARINE (2 STICKS), SOFTENED

2 CUPS SUGAR

1¼ CUPS MILK

1 TABLESPOON VANILLA EXTRACT

8 LARGE EGG WHITES

8 SQUARES (8 OUNCES) SEMISWEET CHOCOLATE, MELTED AND COOLED

CHOCOLATE BUTTERCREAM FROSTING (PAGE 63)

1 Preheat oven to 350°F. Grease three 8-inch round cake pans. Line bottoms of cake pans with waxed paper; grease paper. Dust with flour (page 45).

2 In medium bowl, combine flour, baking powder, and salt.

3 In large bowl, with mixer at low speed, beat butter and 1½ cups sugar until blended. Increase speed to high; beat until light and fluffy, about 5 minutes. Reduce speed to low. Add flour mixture, milk, and vanilla; beat until just combined. Increase speed to medium; beat 2 minutes, occasionally scraping bowl.

4 In separate large bowl, with mixer at high speed, beat egg whites until soft peaks form when beaters are lifted. Sprinkle in remaining ½ cup sugar, 2 tablespoons at a time, beating until sugar has dissolved and whites stand in stiff, glossy peaks. Do not overbeat. Gently fold egg whites, one-third at a time, into flour mixture until blended. Spoon half of batter into medium bowl. Into batter still in large bowl, fold in chocolate until blended.

5 Spoon vanilla batter into large pastry bag with ½-inch opening (or a heavy-duty plastic bag with corner cut to make ½-inch opening). Spoon chocolate batter into separate pastry bag with ½-inch opening. Pipe 1½-inch-wide band of chocolate batter around inside edge of two pans. Pipe 1½-inch-wide band of vanilla next to each chocolate band. Pipe in enough chocolate to fill center. In third cake pan, pipe alternating rings of batter, but starting with vanilla band around edge of pan.

6 Bake until toothpick inserted in center comes out clean, 25 to 30 minutes. Cool in pans on wire racks 10 minutes. Run thin knife around sides to loosen from pans. Invert onto racks. Remove waxed paper; cool completely.

7 Meanwhile, prepare Chocolate Buttercream Frosting.

8 Place one of the two identical cake layers, rounded side down, on cake plate. With narrow metal spatula, spread ½ cup buttercream over layer. Top with reverse-design cake layer, rounded side up, and spread with ½ cup buttercream. Place remaining cake layer, rounded side up, on top. Spread remaining buttercream over side and top of cake.

EACH SERVING: ABOUT 585 CALORIES | 6G PROTEIN | 78G CARBOHYDRATE | 29G TOTAL FAT (10G SATURATED) | 2G FIBER | 34MG CHOLESTEROL | 459MG SODIUM

TRIPLE-CHOCOLATE FUDGE CAKE

Dusting the cake pan with cocoa instead of flour prevents white streaks from forming on the outside of the cake. See page 45 for photo of technique. If your cocoa has been sitting in your pantry for a while, press it through a strainer or sifter to remove any lumps.

ACTIVE TIME: 1 HOUR · **TOTAL TIME:** 1 HOUR 45 MINUTES PLUS COOLING
MAKES: 16 SERVINGS

CAKE

1	CUP ALL-PURPOSE FLOUR
⅓	CUP UNSWEETENED COCOA
½	TEASPOON SALT
8	SQUARES (8 OUNCES) SEMISWEET CHOCOLATE, CHOPPED
½	CUP BUTTER OR MARGARINE (1 STICK)
1	TEASPOON INSTANT-COFFEE POWDER OR GRANULES
¼	CUP HOT WATER
6	LARGE EGGS, SEPARATED
¼	TEASPOON CREAM OF TARTAR
1	CUP SUGAR
1½	TEASPOONS VANILLA EXTRACT

CHOCOLATE GLAZE

½	CUP SEMISWEET CHOCOLATE CHIPS
2	TABLESPOONS BUTTER OR MARGARINE
3	TABLESPOONS MILK
2	TABLESPOONS LIGHT CORN SYRUP

CHOCOLATE DRIZZLES

1	BAR (1½ TO 2 OUNCES) MILK CHOCOLATE
2	TEASPOONS VEGETABLE SHORTENING
2	OUNCES WHITE CHOCOLATE

1 Preheat oven to 375°F. Grease 9" by 3" springform pan. Line bottom with waxed paper; grease paper. Dust with cocoa (page 45). Wrap outside of pan with heavy-duty foil to prevent water from leaking in during baking.
2 In medium bowl, combine flour, cocoa, and salt. In small saucepan, melt semisweet chocolate and butter over low heat, stirring frequently until smooth. In cup, dissolve instant-coffee powder in hot water.
3 In small bowl, with mixer at high speed, beat egg whites and cream of tartar until soft peaks form when beaters are lifted. Sprinkle in ½ cup sugar, 2 tablespoons at a time, beating until sugar has dissolved and egg whites stand in stiff, glossy peaks when beaters are lifted. Do not overbeat.

4 In large bowl, with mixer at high speed, beat egg yolks and remaining ½ cup sugar until thick and lemon-colored, about 10 minutes. Reduce speed to low. Stir in flour mixture, chocolate mixture, coffee mixture, and vanilla until blended. With rubber spatula, gently fold in beaten egg whites. Pour batter into prepared pan.

5 Set springform pan in medium roasting pan. Fill roasting pan with enough boiling water to reach halfway up sides of pan. Bake the cake 45 minutes (center will still be slightly soft). Remove springform pan from roasting pan. Cool cake in springform pan on wire rack. Remove side of springform pan; invert cake onto cake plate. Remove bottom of pan and waxed paper.

6 Prepare Chocolate Glaze: In 2-quart saucepan, melt chocolate chips and butter over low heat, stirring often until smooth. Remove from heat; stir in milk and corn syrup until blended. With narrow metal spatula, spread warm glaze over top of cooled cake, allowing it to run down side of cake.

7 Prepare Chocolate Drizzles: In 1-quart saucepan, melt milk chocolate and 1 teaspoon shortening over low heat, stirring often, until smooth. Spoon into small ziptight plastic bag. Wash and dry pan. In same clean pan, melt white chocolate and remaining 1 teaspoon shortening over low heat, stirring often, until smooth. Spoon white-chocolate mixture into separate small ziptight plastic bag. Cut very small hole in corner of each plastic bag. Drizzle milk and white chocolates over top of cake. Pull tip of knife or toothpick through chocolates to make decorative design.

8 To serve, dip knife into hot water and dry immediately (the heated blade will cut through the cake without sticking). Cut cake into wedges.

EACH SERVING: ABOUT 320 CALORIES | 6G PROTEIN | 36G CARBOHYDRATE | 18G TOTAL FAT (6G SATURATED) | 2G FIBER | 81MG CHOLESTEROL | 205MG SODIUM

SACHER TORTE

This decadent Viennese chocolate dessert has two layers of apricot preserves and is covered with a chocolate glaze. Be traditional and serve the cake with *schlag* (whipped cream). And, of course, for the best results, use butter, not margarine.

ACTIVE TIME: 45 MINUTES · **TOTAL TIME:** 1 HOUR 25 MINUTES PLUS COOLING
MAKES: 10 SERVINGS

CAKE

- ¾ CUP BUTTER (1½ STICKS), SOFTENED (DO NOT USE MARGARINE)
- ¾ CUP CONFECTIONERS' SUGAR
- 6 LARGE EGGS, SEPARATED
- 1 TEASPOON VANILLA EXTRACT
- 3 SQUARES (3 OUNCES) UNSWEETENED CHOCOLATE, CHOPPED
- 3 SQUARES (3 OUNCES) SEMISWEET CHOCOLATE, CHOPPED
- ¼ TEASPOON SALT
- ¼ TEASPOON CREAM OF TARTAR
- ½ CUP GRANULATED SUGAR
- ¾ CUP ALL-PURPOSE FLOUR
- 1 CUP APRICOT PRESERVES

CHOCOLATE GLAZE

- 3 SQUARES (3 OUNCES) SEMISWEET CHOCOLATE, CHOPPED
- 2 TABLESPOONS BUTTER
- 1 TEASPOON LIGHT CORN SYRUP

1 Preheat oven to 350°F. Grease 9-inch springform pan. Line bottom of pan with waxed paper; grease paper. Dust pan with flour (page 45).

2 In large bowl, with mixer at medium speed, beat butter and confectioners' sugar until light and fluffy, about 3 minutes. Beat in egg yolks and vanilla until well blended.

3 In heavy 1-quart saucepan, melt unsweetened and semisweet chocolates over low heat, stirring often, until smooth. With mixer at medium speed, immediately beat melted chocolate into egg-yolk mixture until well blended. (Chocolate must be warm, about 130°F, when added to egg-yolk mixture, or batter will be too stiff.) Wash and dry beaters.

4 In medium bowl, with clean beaters and with mixer at high speed, beat egg whites, salt, and cream of tartar until soft peaks form when beaters are lifted. Sprinkle in granulated sugar, 2 tablespoons at a time, beating until sugar has dissolved and egg whites stand in stiff, glossy peaks when beaters are lifted. Do not overbeat. With rubber spatula, gently fold beaten egg whites, one-third at a time, into chocolate mixture until blended. Sift flour, about ¼ cup at a time, over chocolate mixture; gently fold in just until blended.

5 Scrape batter into prepared pan; spread evenly. Bake until toothpick inserted in center comes out clean, 40 to 45 minutes. Cool in pan on wire rack 10 minutes. Run thin knife around cake to loosen from side of pan; remove pan side. Invert cake onto rack. Slip knife under cake to separate from bottom of pan; remove pan bottom. Remove waxed paper; cool cake completely on rack.

6 When cake is cool, with serrated knife, cut horizontally into two layers. Place one layer, cut side up, on cake plate. In 1-quart saucepan, heat apricot preserves over medium-high heat until melted and bubbling. Strain through sieve set over small bowl. With pastry brush, brush half of preserves evenly over layer; replace top layer and spread evenly with remaining preserves. Let stand 10 minutes to set preserves slightly.

7 Meanwhile, prepare Chocolate Glaze: In heavy 1-quart saucepan, heat chocolate, butter, and corn syrup over low heat, stirring frequently, until chocolate and butter have melted and mixture is smooth. Remove from heat and cool slightly, about 5 minutes.

8 Pour glaze over cake. With narrow metal spatula, spread glaze, allowing some to drip down side of cake; completely cover top and side of cake. Let stand 30 minutes to allow glaze to set. If not serving right away, refrigerate up to 4 hours. Let cake stand 20 minutes at room temperature before serving.

EACH SERVING: ABOUT 505 CALORIES | 7G PROTEIN | 61G CARBOHYDRATE | 29G TOTAL FAT (17G SATURATED) | 3G FIBER | 171MG CHOLESTEROL | 276MG SODIUM

BLACK FOREST CAKE

Our luscious three-layer chocolate extravaganza filled with cherries and kirsch-laced whipped cream celebrates two of Germany's glories: cherries from the Black Forest region and the brandy distilled from them.

ACTIVE TIME: 1 HOUR · **TOTAL TIME:** 1 HOUR 25 MINUTES PLUS COOLING
MAKES: 16 SERVINGS

CHOCOLATE CAKE

2 CUPS ALL-PURPOSE FLOUR

1 CUP UNSWEETENED COCOA

2 TEASPOONS BAKING POWDER

1 TEASPOON BAKING SODA

½ TEASPOON SALT

1⅓ CUPS MILK

2 TEASPOONS VANILLA EXTRACT

1 CUP BUTTER OR MARGARINE (2 STICKS), SOFTENED

2 CUPS SUGAR

4 LARGE EGGS

CHERRY FILLING

2 CANS (16½ OUNCES EACH) PITTED DARK SWEET CHERRIES (BING) IN HEAVY SYRUP

⅓ CUP KIRSCH (CHERRY BRANDY)

CREAM FILLING

1½ CUPS HEAVY OR WHIPPING CREAM

½ CUP CONFECTIONERS' SUGAR

2 TABLESPOONS KIRSCH (CHERRY BRANDY)

1 TEASPOON VANILLA EXTRACT

CHOCOLATE CURLS (PAGE 166)

1 Preheat oven to 350°F. Grease three 9-inch round cake pans. Line bottoms with waxed paper; grease paper. Dust pans with cocoa (page 45).

2 Prepare Chocolate Cake: In medium bowl, combine flour, cocoa, baking powder, baking soda, and salt. In measuring cup, mix milk and vanilla.

3 In large bowl, with mixer at low speed, beat butter and sugar until blended. Increase speed to high; beat until creamy, about 2 minutes. Reduce speed to medium-low; add eggs, one at a time, beating well after each addition. Add flour mixture alternately with milk mixture, beginning and ending with flour mixture, beating until batter is smooth, occasionally scraping bowl with rubber spatula.

4 Divide batter among cake pans; spread evenly. Place two cake pans on upper oven rack and one on lower oven rack so pans are not directly above one another. Bake until toothpick inserted in center comes out almost clean, about 25 minutes. Cool in pans on wire racks 10 minutes. Run thin knife around layers to loosen from sides of pans. Invert onto racks. Remove waxed paper; cool completely.

5 Meanwhile, prepare Cherry Filling: Drain cherries well in sieve set over bowl. Reserve ½ cup syrup; stir kirsch into syrup.

6 Prepare Cream Filling: In small bowl, with mixer at medium speed, beat cream, confectioners' sugar, kirsch, and vanilla until stiff peaks form.

7 Place one cake layer, rounded side down, on cake plate. Brush with one-third of syrup mixture. With narrow metal spatula, spread one-third of whipped-cream mixture over layer, top with half of cherries. Top with second cake layer, rounded side up. Brush with half of remaining syrup mixture, spread with half of remaining cream mixture, and top with remaining cherries. Place remaining layer, rounded side up, on top; brush with remaining syrup mixture. Spoon remaining cream mixture onto center of top layer, leaving a border.

8 Pile chocolate curls on top of whipped cream. Refrigerate overnight.

EACH SERVING: ABOUT 450 CALORIES | 6G PROTEIN | 58G CARBOHYDRATE | 22G TOTAL FAT (13G SATURATED) | 3G FIBER | 118MG CHOLESTEROL | 344MG SODIUM

CHOCOLATE GÉNOISE WITH GANACHE

Cakes don't get more elegant than a génoise covered with rich and creamy ganache. We recommend using a high-quality chocolate for the most decadent ganache.

ACTIVE TIME: 50 MINUTES · **TOTAL TIME:** 1 HOUR 15 MINUTES PLUS COOLING
MAKES: 20 SERVINGS

7 LARGE EGGS	½ TEASPOON SALT
1¼ CUPS GRANULATED SUGAR	½ CUP BUTTER OR MARGARINE (1 STICK), MELTED AND COOLED TO LUKEWARM
1½ TEASPOONS VANILLA EXTRACT	
¾ CUP CAKE FLOUR (NOT SELF-RISING)	GANACHE (PAGE 75)
¾ CUP UNSWEETENED COCOA	CONFECTIONERS' SUGAR

1 Preheat oven to 350°F. Grease two 9-inch round cake pans. Line bottoms with waxed paper; grease paper. Dust pans with cocoa (page 45).

2 In large bowl, with mixer at high speed, beat eggs, granulated sugar, and vanilla until mixture has increased in volume about four times and is the consistency of whipped cream. This will take up to 35 minutes.

3 In medium bowl, combine flour, cocoa, and salt. Sift flour mixture one-fourth at a time, over egg mixture, and gently fold in.

4 Divide batter equally between prepared pans. Bake until cake springs back when lightly touched, about 25 minutes. Cool in pans on wire racks 10 minutes. Run thin knife around layers to loosen from sides of pans. Invert onto racks. Remove waxed paper; cool.

5 Meanwhile, prepare ganache; let stand at room temperature 30 minutes.

6 With serrated knife, cut each cake layer horizontally in half. Place bottom half of one layer, cut side up, on cake plate. With narrow metal spatula spread with ⅓ cup ganache. Top with second layer, rounded side up, and spread with ⅓ cup ganache. Repeat layering to make 4 layers of cake and 3 layers of ganache in all. Dust cake with confectioners' sugar; spread remaining ganache on side of cake.

EACH SERVING: ABOUT 260 CALORIES | 4G PROTEIN | 29G CARBOHYDRATE | 16G TOTAL FAT (9G SATURATED) | 2G FIBER | 104MG CHOLESTEROL | 140MG SODIUM

CHOCOLATE NEMESIS

This silky flourless cake is a showstopper. Whipped cream and fresh raspberries on top increase the wow factor.

ACTIVE TIME: 35 MINUTES · **TOTAL TIME:** 1 HOUR 5 MINUTES PLUS COOLING
MAKES: 16 SERVINGS

½ CUP WATER

1 CUP SUGAR

1 POUND BITTERSWEET CHOCOLATE (GOOD QUALITY), CHOPPED

1 CUP UNSALTED BUTTER (2 STICKS), CUT UP (DO NOT USE MARGARINE)

7 LARGE EGGS

SOFTLY WHIPPED CREAM OR CRÈME FRAÎCHE

FRESH RASPBERRIES

1 Preheat oven to 325°F. Grease bottom and side of 9-inch springform pan. Dust side of pan with cocoa (page 45). Set pan on wide sheet of heavy-duty foil and tightly wrap outside of pan to prevent water from leaking in during baking.

2 In 4-quart saucepan, heat water and ½ cup sugar over medium-high heat until sugar completely dissolves, stirring occasionally. Add chocolate and butter to mixture in saucepan; stir constantly until melted. Remove from heat and allow to cool slightly.

3 Meanwhile, in large bowl, with mixer at high speed, beat eggs with remaining ½ cup sugar 6 to 8 minutes or until mixture thickens and triples in volume. With wire whisk, fold warm chocolate mixture into egg mixture until completely blended.

4 Pour batter into prepared springform pan; place in large (17" by 11½") roasting pan and set on oven rack. Pour enough boiling water into roasting pan to come halfway up side of springform pan.

5 Bake cake 30 to 35 minutes or until edge begins to set and a thin crust forms on top. Carefully remove springform pan from water bath and place on wire rack. Cool cake to room temperature. Cover and refrigerate overnight.

6 About 30 minutes before serving, run sharp knife around edge of pan to loosen cake; remove foil and side of pan. Invert cake onto waxed paper; peel off parchment. Turn cake right side up onto platter. Serve with whipped cream and berries.

EACH SERVING: ABOUT 345 CALORIES | 5G PROTEIN | 22G CARBOHYDRATE | 27G TOTAL FAT (15G SATURATED) | 1G FIBER | 126MG CHOLESTEROL | 45MG SODIUM

FABULOUS FLOURLESS CHOCOLATE CAKE

This exceptionally sinful chocolate dessert is easy to make, but it must be refrigerated for twenty-four hours before serving for the best flavor and texture. For the neatest slices, dip the knife into hot water before cutting each one.

ACTIVE TIME: 1 HOUR · **TOTAL TIME:** 1 HOUR 35 MINUTES PLUS COOLING
MAKES: 20 SERVINGS

---

14 SQUARES (14 OUNCES) SEMISWEET CHOCOLATE, CHOPPED

2 SQUARES (2 OUNCES) UNSWEETENED CHOCOLATE, CHOPPED

1 CUP BUTTER (2 STICKS, DO NOT USE MARGARINE)

9 LARGE EGGS, SEPARATED

½ CUP GRANULATED SUGAR

¼ TEASPOON CREAM OF TARTAR

CONFECTIONERS' SUGAR

1 Preheat oven to 300°F. Remove bottom of 9" by 3" springform pan; cover disk with foil, wrapping foil around back. Replace pan bottom. Grease foil bottom and side of pan and dust with cocoa (page 45).

2 In heavy 2-quart saucepan, melt semisweet and unsweetened chocolates and butter over low heat, stirring frequently, until smooth. Pour chocolate mixture into large bowl.

3 In small bowl, with mixer at high speed, beat egg yolks and granulated sugar until very thick and lemon-colored, about 10 minutes. With rubber spatula, stir egg-yolk mixture into chocolate mixture until blended. Wash and dry beaters.

4 In separate large bowl, with clean beaters and with mixer at high speed, beat egg whites and cream of tartar until soft peaks form when beaters are lifted. With rubber spatula, gently fold beaten egg whites, one-third at a time, into chocolate mixture just until blended.

5 Scrape batter into prepared pan; spread evenly. Bake 35 minutes. (Do not overbake; cake will firm upon standing and chilling.) Cool completely in pan on wire rack; refrigerate overnight in pan.

6 Run thin knife, rinsed under very hot water and dried, around cake to loosen from side of pan; remove side of pan. Invert onto cake plate; unwrap foil from pan bottom and lift off disk. Carefully peel foil away from cake.

7 To serve, let cake stand at room temperature 1 hour. Dust with confectioners' sugar. Or dust heavily with confectioners' sugar over paper doily or stencil (page 170).

EACH SERVING: ABOUT 245 CALORIES | 4G PROTEIN | 19G CARBOHYDRATE | 19G TOTAL FAT
(11G SATURATED) | 2G FIBER | 120MG CHOLESTEROL | 125MG SODIUM

FLOURLESS CHOCOLATE-HAZELNUT CAKE

In 1984, a gooey gâteau au chocolat kicked off *Good Housekeeping*'s long-running love affair with flour-free cakes. This recipe is almost identical to that fudgy forerunner—with one important change: A generous portion of hazelnuts is folded into the batter, which adds a delectable depth of flavor.

ACTIVE TIME: 30 MINUTES · **TOTAL TIME:** 1 HOUR 15 MINUTES PLUS COOLING
MAKES: 12 SERVINGS

¾ CUP HAZELNUTS (4 OUNCES)

¾ CUP GRANULATED SUGAR

8 SQUARES (8 OUNCES) SEMISWEET CHOCOLATE, CHOPPED

4 TABLESPOONS BUTTER OR MARGARINE, SOFTENED

5 LARGE EGGS

¾ CUP HEAVY OR WHIPPING CREAM

1 TABLESPOON CONFECTIONERS' SUGAR

1 Preheat oven to 350°F. Lightly grease 9-inch springform pan. Line bottom with waxed paper; grease paper.

2 Place hazelnuts in 15½" by 10½" jelly-roll pan. Bake 10 to 15 minutes or until toasted and fragrant, shaking pan occasionally. Wrap hot hazelnuts in clean cloth towel; with hands, roll hazelnuts back and forth until as much skin as possible rubs off. Cool nuts completely.

3 In food processor with knife blade attached, place nuts and ¼ cup granulated sugar; pulse until finely ground.

4 In 3-quart saucepan, melt chocolate and butter on medium-low, stirring occasionally. Meanwhile, in large bowl, with mixer on medium-high speed, beat eggs and remaining ½ cup granulated sugar 7 minutes or until tripled in volume. With rubber spatula, fold in chocolate mixture, then fold in ground-nut mixture. Pour batter into prepared pan and bake 35 minutes or until top is dry and cracked and toothpick inserted in center comes out slightly wet. Cool in pan on wire rack 10 minutes. Remove side of pan and cool 30 minutes longer on rack.

5 In large bowl, with mixer on medium speed, beat cream until soft peaks form, 3 to 5 minutes.

6 To serve, place confectioners' sugar in fine mesh sieve. Sprinkle over cake. Cut cake into 12 slices and divide them among serving plates. Top each slice with dollop of whipped cream.

EACH SERVING: ABOUT 315 CALORIES | 6G PROTEIN | 25G CARBOHYDRATE | 123G TOTAL FAT (10G SATURATED) | 2G FIBER | 20MG CHOLESTEROL | 75MG SODIUM

CHOCOLATE, PRUNE, AND NUT TORTE

The combination of chocolate, prunes, and pecans may seem unlikely, but they are a classic—and delicious—combination. Rich-tasting pecans work well here, but walnuts are also a good choice.

ACTIVE TIME: 1 HOUR · **TOTAL TIME:** 1 HOUR 35 MINUTES PLUS OVERNIGHT TO CHILL
MAKES: 12 SERVINGS

---

3 BITTERSWEET CHOCOLATE BARS (3 OUNCES EACH) OR 9 SQUARES (9 OUNCES) SEMISWEET CHOCOLATE

6 LARGE EGG WHITES

½ CUP GRANULATED SUGAR

½ TEASPOON VANILLA EXTRACT

2 CUPS PITTED PRUNES (ABOUT 10 OUNCES), DICED

1½ CUPS PECANS (6 OUNCES), COARSELY CHOPPED

1 TABLESPOON CONFECTIONERS' SUGAR

1 Grease 10" by 2½" springform pan; line bottom of pan with waxed paper.
2 Finely grate chocolate. (Or, in food processor with knife blade attached, process chocolate until ground.)
3 Preheat oven to 425°F. In large bowl, with mixer at high speed, beat egg whites until soft peaks form when beaters are lifted. Sprinkle in granulated sugar, 2 tablespoons at a time, beating until sugar has dissolved and egg whites stand in stiff, glossy peaks when beaters are lifted. Beat in vanilla.
4 With rubber spatula, gently fold prunes and pecans into beaten egg whites; gently but thoroughly fold in grated chocolate. Pour into prepared pan; spread evenly. Bake until top of torte is deep brown and torte pulls away from side of pan, about 35 minutes.
5 Cool torte in pan on wire rack 15 minutes; remove side of pan. Invert torte and remove bottom of pan; remove waxed paper. Cool completely on rack. Cover and refrigerate overnight.
6 Just before serving, cut six 12" by ½" strips of waxed paper. Place strips, 1 inch apart, on top of torte to create a striped pattern. Dust torte with confectioners' sugar, then carefully lift off waxed-paper strips. Refrigerate any leftover torte.

EACH SERVING: ABOUT 305 CALORIES | 6G PROTEIN | 34G CARBOHYDRATE | 21G TOTAL FAT (7G SATURATED) | 4G FIBER | 0MG CHOLESTEROL | 30MG SODIUM

CHOCOLATE-BOURBON POUND CAKE

Make sure to use the traditional Bundt pan for this cake.

ACTIVE TIME: 30 MINUTES · **TOTAL TIME:** 1 HOUR 40 MINUTES PLUS COOLING

MAKES: 24 SERVINGS

CHOCOLATE CAKE

2½ CUPS ALL-PURPOSE FLOUR

1 CUP UNSWEETENED COCOA

½ TEASPOON BAKING POWDER

½ TEASPOON SALT

¼ CUP BOURBON

2 TEASPOONS VANILLA EXTRACT

1 TEASPOON INSTANT ESPRESSO-COFFEE POWDER

1¼ CUPS (2½ STICKS) BUTTER OR MARGARINE, SOFTENED

2¾ CUPS GRANULATED SUGAR

5 LARGE EGGS

1¼ CUPS WHOLE MILK

2 OUNCES BITTERSWEET OR SEMISWEET CHOCOLATE, GRATED

BROWN SUGAR GLAZE

⅓ CUP PACKED LIGHT BROWN SUGAR

4 TABLESPOONS BUTTER OR MARGARINE

3 TABLESPOONS BOURBON

1 CUP CONFECTIONERS' SUGAR

1 Preheat oven to 350°F. Grease and flour 12-cup Bundt pan (page 45). In medium bowl, combine flour, cocoa, baking powder, and salt. In liquid measuring cup, mix bourbon, vanilla, and espresso powder well; set aside.

2 In large bowl, with mixer at medium speed, beat butter until creamy. Gradually beat in granulated sugar, scraping bowl often with rubber spatula. Beat in bourbon mixture. Reduce speed to low; add eggs, one at a time, beating well after each addition.

3 With mixer at low speed, alternately add flour mixture and milk, beginning and ending with flour mixture, until batter is blended. Beat in grated chocolate. Spoon batter into Bundt pan, spreading evenly.

4 Bake cake about 1 hour and 10 minutes or until toothpick inserted in center of cake comes out clean. Cool cake in pan on wire rack 10 minutes. Invert cake onto wire rack to cool completely.

5 Prepare glaze: Place cooled cake on plate. In 2-quart saucepan, heat brown sugar and butter over medium heat until bubbly, about 3 minutes, stirring often. Remove from heat. With wire whisk, beat in bourbon and confectioners' sugar until smooth. Immediately pour glaze over top of cake, letting it run down sides. Allow glaze to set before serving.

EACH SERVING: ABOUT 320 CALORIES | 4G PROTEIN | 44G CARBOHYDRATE | 15G TOTAL FAT (16G SATURATED) | 2G FIBER | 79MG CHOLESTEROL | 205MG SODIUM

CHOCOLATE POUND CAKE WITH IRISH WHISKEY– CREAM SAUCE

This dense, decadent chocolate Bundt cake can also be served with a big dollop of vanilla- or rum-flavored whipped cream.

ACTIVE TIME: 30 MINUTES · **TOTAL TIME:** 1 HOUR 45 MINUTES PLUS COOLING
MAKES: 20 SERVINGS

CHOCOLATE CAKE

3   CUPS ALL-PURPOSE FLOUR

1   CUP UNSWEETENED COCOA

½   TEASPOON BAKING POWDER

1½ CUPS BUTTER OR MARGARINE (3 STICKS), SOFTENED

2¾ CUPS GRANULATED SUGAR

2   TEASPOONS VANILLA EXTRACT

5   LARGE EGGS

1½ CUPS MILK

2   OUNCES BITTERSWEET CHOCOLATE OR 2 SQUARES (2 OUNCES) SEMISWEET CHOCOLATE, GRATED

IRISH WHISKEY–CREAM SAUCE

1   CUP HEAVY OR WHIPPING CREAM

⅓   CUP CONFECTIONERS' SUGAR PLUS ADDITIONAL FOR DUSTING CAKE

¼   CUP FRESHLY BREWED COFFEE

2   TABLESPOONS IRISH WHISKEY OR BOURBON

1 Prepare Chocolate Cake: Preheat oven to 350°F. Grease and flour 12-cup Bundt pan (oppostite). In medium bowl, combine flour, cocoa, and baking powder.

2 In large bowl, with mixer at medium speed, beat butter until creamy. Gradually beat in granulated sugar, frequently scraping bowl with rubber spatula. Beat 3 minutes, occasionally scraping bowl. Beat in vanilla. Reduce speed to low; add eggs, one at a time, beating well after each addition. Add flour mixture alternately with milk, beginning and ending with flour mixture. Beat just until batter is blended, occasionally scraping bowl. Stir in grated chocolate.

3 Spoon batter into prepared pan; spread evenly. Bake until toothpick inserted in center of cake comes out clean, 1 hour 15 minutes. Cool cake in pan on wire rack 10 minutes. Invert cake onto wire rack to cool completely.

DUSTING PAN WITH FLOUR

Using a piece of folded paper towel or waxed paper, spread a thin layer of shortening inside the baking pan. Sprinkle about 1 tablespoon flour into the pan. Tilt to coat the bottom and side with the flour; invert the pan and tap out the excess flour. For chocolate cakes that won't be frosted or glazed, substitute unsweetened cocoa for the flour. The cocoa will be invisible on the chocolate cake.

4 Meanwhile, prepare Irish Whiskey–Cream Sauce: In small bowl, with mixer at low speed, beat cream until frothy. Add confectioners' sugar; increase speed to medium and beat until stiff peaks form. With rubber spatula or wire whisk, fold in coffee and whiskey until blended; cover and refrigerate up to 4 hours. Makes about 2 cups.

5 To serve, dust cake with confectioners' sugar. Cut cake into wedges and pass cream sauce to spoon over each serving.

EACH SERVING WITHOUT SAUCE: ABOUT 350 CALORIES | 5G PROTEIN | 47G CARBOHYDRATE
17G TOTAL FAT (5G SATURATED) | 2G FIBER | 93MG CHOLESTEROL | 177MG SODIUM

EACH TABLESPOON SAUCE: ABOUT 35 CALORIES | 0G PROTEIN | 1G CARBOHYDRATE
3G TOTAL FAT (2G SATURATED) | 2G FIBER | 10MG CHOLESTEROL | 5MG SODIUM

DOUBLE-CHOCOLATE BUNDT CAKE

This lowfat cake will satisfy a chocolate craving. If you use a dusting of confectioners' sugar instead of the glaze, you'll save thirty-five calories per slice.

ACTIVE TIME: 30 MINUTES · **TOTAL TIME:** 1 HOUR 15 MINUTES PLUS COOLING

MAKES: 20 SERVINGS

2¼ CUPS ALL-PURPOSE FLOUR

1½ TEASPOONS BAKING SODA

½ TEASPOON BAKING POWDER

½ TEASPOON SALT

¾ CUP UNSWEETENED COCOA

1 TEASPOON INSTANT ESPRESSO-COFFEE POWDER

¾ CUP HOT WATER

2 CUPS SUGAR

⅓ CUP VEGETABLE OIL

2 LARGE EGG WHITES

1 LARGE EGG

1 SQUARE (1 OUNCE) UNSWEETENED CHOCOLATE, MELTED

2 TEASPOONS VANILLA EXTRACT

½ CUP BUTTERMILK

MOCHA GLAZE (PAGE 74)

1 Preheat oven to 350°F. Generously spray 12-cup Bundt pan with nonstick cooking spray.

2 In medium bowl, combine flour, baking soda, baking powder, and salt.

3 In measuring cup, whisk cocoa and espresso-coffee powder into hot water until blended.

4 In large bowl, with mixer at low speed, beat sugar, oil, egg whites, and egg until blended. Increase speed to high; beat until creamy, about 2 minutes. Reduce speed to low; beat in cocoa mixture, melted chocolate, and vanilla until blended. Add flour mixture alternately with buttermilk, beginning and ending with flour mixture. Beat just until blended, occasionally scraping bowl with rubber spatula.

5 Pour batter into prepared pan. Bake until toothpick inserted in center comes out clean, about 45 minutes. Cool cake in pan on wire rack 10 minutes. Run tip of knife around edge of cake to loosen from side of pan; invert onto rack to cool completely.

6 Prepare Mocha Glaze. Pour over cooled cake.

EACH SERVING: ABOUT 220 CALORIES | 3G PROTEIN | 43G CARBOHYDRATE | 5G TOTAL FAT (1G SATURATED) | 2G FIBER | 11MG CHOLESTEROL | 175MG SODIUM

TRIPLE-CHOCOLATE CHERRY CAKE

You can make this delectable cake and stash it—well wrapped—in the freezer for up to one month. Then let it thaw, still in its wrapping, at room temperature before serving.

ACTIVE TIME: 40 MINUTES · **TOTAL TIME:** 1 HOUR 40 MINUTES PLUS COOLING
MAKES: 16 SERVINGS

1¾ CUPS ALL-PURPOSE FLOUR

¾ CUP UNSWEETENED COCOA

1½ TEASPOONS BAKING SODA

½ TEASPOON SALT

1 CUP DRIED TART CHERRIES

1 TABLESPOON INSTANT ESPRESSO-COFFEE POWDER

1 TABLESPOON VERY HOT WATER

1½ CUPS BUTTERMILK

2 TEASPOONS VANILLA EXTRACT

1 CUP BUTTER (2 STICKS), SOFTENED (DO NOT USE MARGARINE)

1¾ CUPS SUGAR

3 LARGE EGGS

2 SQUARES (2 OUNCES) UNSWEETENED CHOCOLATE, MELTED

1 PACKAGE (6 OUNCES) SEMISWEET CHOCOLATE CHIPS

CONFECTIONERS' SUGAR

WHIPPED CREAM (OPTIONAL)

1 Preheat oven to 325°F. Grease and flour 10-inch Bundt pan (page 45).

2 In medium bowl, combine flour, cocoa, baking soda, and salt.

3 In small bowl, combine cherries with enough very hot water to cover; let stand at least 5 minutes to soften cherries. In measuring cup, dissolve espresso powder in 1 tablespoon hot water; stir in buttermilk and vanilla.

4 In large bowl, with mixer at low speed, beat butter and sugar until blended, frequently scraping bowl with rubber spatula. Increase speed to medium; beat 2 minutes, occasionally scraping bowl. Reduce speed to low; add eggs, one at a time, beating well after each addition. At low speed, alternately add flour mixture and buttermilk mixture, beginning and ending with flour mixture; beat until smooth, occasionally scraping bowl.

5 Drain cherries and pat dry with paper towels. With rubber spatula, fold melted unsweetened chocolate into batter; fold in chocolate chips and drained cherries.

6 Pour batter into prepared pan. Bake until toothpick inserted in center comes out clean, 1 hour to 1 hour 10 minutes. Cool cake in pan on wire rack 10 minutes. Invert cake onto rack to cool completely.

7 To serve, dust confectioners' sugar over cake. Pass whipped cream separately, if you like.

EACH SERVING WITHOUT WHIPPED CREAM: ABOUT 365 CALORIES │ 5G PROTEIN
52G CARBOHYDRATE │ 17G TOTAL FAT (8G SATURATED) │ 5G FIBER │ 72MG CHOLESTEROL
345MG SODIUM

WARM CHOCOLATE BANANA CAKE

Chocolate lovers won't feel deprived when they dig into this lowfat brownie-like cake with a fudgy texture. Serve with fat-free vanilla ice cream, if you like.

ACTIVE TIME: 15 MINUTES · **TOTAL TIME:** 50 MINUTES
MAKES: 8 SERVINGS

1 CUP ALL-PURPOSE FLOUR

1 CUP UNSWEETENED COCOA

½ CUP GRANULATED SUGAR

1 TEASPOON BAKING POWDER

½ TEASPOON SALT

¼ TEASPOON GROUND CINNAMON

1 RIPE LARGE BANANA, MASHED (½ CUP)

1 LARGE EGG, BEATEN

¼ CUP COLD WATER PLUS 1¼ CUPS BOILING WATER

2 TABLESPOONS BUTTER OR MARGARINE, MELTED

1 TEASPOON VANILLA EXTRACT

½ CUP PACKED DARK BROWN SUGAR

1 Preheat oven to 350°F. In large bowl, combine flour, ¾ cup cocoa, granulated sugar, baking powder, salt, and cinnamon.

2 In medium bowl, with wooden spoon, stir banana, egg, cold water, butter, and vanilla until blended.

3 Stir banana mixture into flour mixture just until blended (batter will be thick). Spoon into ungreased 8-inch square baking dish; spread evenly.

4 In same large bowl, with wire whisk, beat brown sugar, remaining ¼ cup cocoa, and boiling water until blended. Pour over chocolate batter in baking dish; do not stir.

5 Bake 35 minutes (dessert should have some fudgy sauce on top). Cool in pan on wire rack 5 minutes. Serve warm.

EACH SERVING: ABOUT 235 CALORIES | 5G PROTEIN | 47G CARBOHYDRATE | 5G TOTAL FAT (3G SATURATED) | 4G FIBER | 35MG CHOLESTEROL | 240MG SODIUM

CHOCOLATE ANGEL FOOD CAKE

Here's how to have your chocolate cake and eat it too—with almost no fat! Using cocoa powder instead of solid chocolate makes the magic possible. Serve the cake sprinkled with confectioners' sugar, if you like.

ACTIVE TIME: 30 MINUTES · **TOTAL TIME:** 1 HOUR 5 MINUTES
MAKES: 12 SERVINGS

¾ CUP CAKE FLOUR (NOT SELF-RISING)

½ CUP UNSWEETENED COCOA

1½ CUPS SUGAR

1⅔ CUPS EGG WHITES
(12 TO 14 LARGE EGG WHITES)

1½ TEASPOONS CREAM OF TARTAR

½ TEASPOON SALT

1½ TEASPOONS VANILLA EXTRACT

1 Preheat oven to 375°F. Sift flour, cocoa, and ¾ cup sugar through sieve set over medium bowl.

2 In large bowl, with mixer at medium speed, beat egg whites, cream of tartar, and salt until foamy (page 53). Increase speed to medium-high; beat until soft peaks form when beaters are lifted. Gradually sprinkle in remaining ¾ cup sugar, 2 tablespoons at a time, beating until sugar has dissolved and egg whites stand in stiff, glossy peaks when beaters are lifted. Do not overbeat. Beat in vanilla.

3 Sift cocoa mixture, one-third at a time, over beaten egg whites; fold in with rubber spatula just until cocoa mixture is no longer visible. Do not overmix.

4 Scrape batter into ungreased 9- to 10-inch tube pan; spread evenly. Bake until cake springs back when lightly touched, 35 to 40 minutes. Invert cake in pan onto upturned metal funnel or bottleneck to keep top of cake from being compressed; cool completely in pan. Run thin knife around cake to loosen from side and center tube of pan. Remove from pan and place upright on cake plate.

EACH SERVING: ABOUT 150 CALORIES | 5G PROTEIN | 33G CARBOHYDRATE | 1G TOTAL FAT (0G SATURATED) | 1G FIBER | 0MG CHOLESTEROL | 155MG SODIUM

FALLEN CHOCOLATE SOUFFLÉ ROLL

A flourless confection with the texture and taste of a chocolate soufflé but without the worry of it collapsing!

ACTIVE TIME: 30 MINUTES · **TOTAL TIME:** 45 MINUTES PLUS COOLING AND CHILLING
MAKES: 16 SERVINGS

- 1   TEASPOON INSTANT ESPRESSO-COFFEE POWDER
- 3   TABLESPOONS HOT WATER
- 5   SQUARES (5 OUNCES) SEMISWEET CHOCOLATE
- 1   SQUARE (1 OUNCE) UNSWEETENED CHOCOLATE
- 6   LARGE EGGS, SEPARATED
- ¾   CUP GRANULATED SUGAR

- 1   TEASPOON VANILLA EXTRACT
- ¾   TEASPOON GROUND CINNAMON
- ¼   TEASPOON SALT
- ⅛   TEASPOON GROUND CLOVES
- 1½ CUPS HEAVY OR WHIPPING CREAM
- ¼   CUP COFFEE-FLAVORED LIQUEUR
- 5   TABLESPOONS CONFECTIONERS' SUGAR PLUS ADDITIONAL FOR DUSTING

1 Preheat oven to 350°F. Grease 15½" by 10½" jelly-roll pan. Line with waxed paper; grease paper. Dust pan with flour (page 45).

2 In cup, dissolve espresso powder in water. In top of double boiler set over simmering water, melt semisweet and unsweetened chocolates with espresso mixture, stirring frequently, until smooth.

3 In large bowl, with mixer at high speed, beat egg whites until soft peaks form when beaters are lifted (opposite). Sprinkle in ¼ cup granulated sugar, 1 tablespoon at a time, beating until sugar has dissolved and egg whites stand in stiff, glossy peaks when beaters are lifted.

4 In small bowl, with mixer at high speed, beat egg yolks with remaining ½ cup granulated sugar until very thick and lemon-colored, about 10 minutes. Reduce speed to low; beat in vanilla, cinnamon, salt, and cloves. With rubber spatula, fold chocolate mixture into yolk mixture until blended. Gently fold one-third of beaten egg whites into chocolate mixture; fold chocolate mixture into remaining egg whites.

5 Scrape batter into prepared pan; spread evenly. Bake until firm to the touch, about 15 minutes. Cover cake with clean, damp kitchen towel; cool in pan on wire rack 30 minutes.

6 In large bowl, with mixer at medium speed, beat cream until soft peaks form. Beat in coffee liqueur and 3 tablespoons confectioners' sugar; beat until stiff peaks form.

BEATING EGG WHITES

The bowl and beaters must be absolutely clean, because even the tiniest bit of fat will prevent peaks from forming. Stainless steel or glass bowls do the best job. For the fullest volume, use egg whites that are at room temperature.

To beat egg whites until "foamy" or "frothy," beat them until they form a mass of tiny clear bubbles. For "soft peaks," beat until the whites form soft, rounded peaks that droop when the beaters are lifted. For "stiff, glossy peaks," beat until the whites hold a peaked shape when the beaters are lifted—they should still be moist. Over-beaten whites look lumpy and watery—there is no way to salvage them. Simply begin again with new whites.

7 Remove towel from cake; sift remaining 2 tablespoons confectioners' sugar over top. Run thin knife around edges of cake to loosen from sides of pan. Cover cake with sheet of foil and a large cookie sheet; invert onto cookie sheet. Carefully remove waxed paper. With narrow metal spatula, spread whipped cream over cake, leaving ½-inch border. Starting from a long side and using foil to help lift cake, roll cake jelly-roll fashion (cake may crack). Place, seam side down, on long platter. Refrigerate at least 1 hour, or until ready to serve. Just before serving, dust with additional confectioners' sugar.

EACH SERVING: ABOUT 215 CALORIES | 4G PROTEIN | 21G CARBOHYDRATE | 14G TOTAL FAT (8G SATURATED) | 1G FIBER | 110MG CHOLESTEROL | 65MG SODIUM

MOLTEN CHOCOLATE CAKES

When you cut into these warm cakes, their delectable molten centers flow out. You can assemble them up to twenty-four hours ahead and refrigerate them, or freeze them for up to two weeks. If you refrigerate the cakes, bake them for ten minutes; if frozen, bake for sixteen minutes. Serve warm with whipped cream or vanilla ice cream, if desired.

ACTIVE TIME: 20 MINUTES · **TOTAL TIME:** 30 MINUTES

MAKES: 8 SERVINGS

4 SQUARES (4 OUNCES) SEMISWEET CHOCOLATE, CHOPPED	¼ CUP ALL-PURPOSE FLOUR
½ CUP BUTTER OR MARGARINE (1 STICK), CUT INTO PIECES	¼ CUP SUGAR
	2 LARGE EGGS
¼ CUP HEAVY OR WHIPPING CREAM	2 LARGE EGG YOLKS
½ TEASPOON VANILLA EXTRACT	WHIPPED CREAM OR VANILLA ICE CREAM (OPTIONAL)

1 Preheat oven to 400°F. Grease eight 6-ounce custard cups. Dust with sugar (page 45).

2 In heavy 3-quart saucepan, combine chocolate, butter, and cream. Heat over low heat, stirring occasionally, until butter and chocolate have melted and mixture is smooth. Remove from heat. Add vanilla; with wire whisk, stir in flour just until mixture is smooth.

3 In medium bowl, with mixer at high speed, beat sugar, eggs, and egg yolks until thick and lemon-colored, about 10 minutes. Fold egg mixture, one-third at a time, into chocolate mixture until blended.

4 Divide batter equally among prepared custard cups. Place cups in jelly-roll pan for easier handling. Bake until edges of cakes are set but center still jiggles, 8 to 9 minutes. Cool in pan on wire rack 3 minutes. Run thin knife around cakes to loosen from sides of cups; invert onto dessert plates. Serve immediately with whipped cream or ice cream, if you like.

EACH SERVING: ABOUT 281 CALORIES | 4G PROTEIN | 20G CARBOHYDRATE | 22G TOTAL FAT (12G SATURATED) | 1G FIBER | 148MG CHOLESTEROL | 139MG SODIUM

RICH CHOCOLATE CUPCAKES

We've topped these cupcakes with our famous Fudge Frosting, but there are lots of other delicious possibilities in the frostings section of this chapter. Or pipe on a generous whipped-cream rosette.

ACTIVE TIME: 15 MINUTES · **TOTAL TIME:** 40 MINUTES PLUS COOLING
MAKES: 24 CUPCAKES

1⅓ CUPS ALL-PURPOSE FLOUR

⅔ CUP UNSWEETENED COCOA

1½ TEASPOONS BAKING POWDER

½ TEASPOON BAKING SODA

½ TEASPOON SALT

1 CUP MILK

1½ TEASPOONS VANILLA EXTRACT

10 TABLESPOONS BUTTER OR MARGARINE (1¼ STICKS), SOFTENED

1⅓ CUPS SUGAR

2 LARGE EGGS

FUDGE FROSTING (PAGE 65, OPTIONAL)

1 Preheat oven to 350°F. Line twenty-four 2½-inch muffin-pan cups with fluted paper liners.

2 In medium bowl, combine flour, cocoa, baking powder, baking soda, and salt. In measuring cup, mix milk and vanilla.

3 In large bowl, with mixer at low speed, beat butter and sugar just until blended. Increase speed to high; beat until mixture is light and creamy, about 3 minutes. Reduce speed to low; add eggs, one at a time, beating well after each addition. Add flour mixture alternately with milk mixture, beginning and ending with flour mixture. Beat just until combined, occasionally scraping bowl with rubber spatula.

4 Spoon batter into muffin-pan cups. Bake until toothpick inserted in center comes out clean, 22 to 25 minutes. Immediately remove cupcakes from pans and cool completely on wire rack.

5 Meanwhile, prepare Fudge Frosting, if you like; use to frost cupcakes.

EACH CUPCAKE: ABOUT 130 CALORIES | 2G PROTEIN | 18G CARBOHYDRATE | 6G TOTAL FAT (4G SATURATED) | 2G FIBER | 33MG CHOLESTEROL | 160MG SODIUM

BLACK-AND-WHITE CUPCAKES

Presented in multiples, these semisweet-and-white-chocolate-frosted cakes are very striking. (For photo, see page 2.) To make a dramatic "black-eyed Susan" cupcake, stir yellow food coloring into about one-quarter cup white-chocolate frosting until it's tinted bright yellow; use a star tip to pipe on petals, then finish with a chocolate center.

ACTIVE TIME: 1 HOUR 30 MINUTES

TOTAL TIME: 1 HOUR 55 MINUTES PLUS COOLING AND DECORATING

MAKES: 24 CUPCAKES

RICH CHOCOLATE CUPCAKES (OPPOSITE)

WHITE CHOCOLATE BUTTERCREAM FROSTING (PAGE 68)

2 SQUARES (2 OUNCES) UNSWEETENED CHOCOLATE, MELTED AND COOLED

1 SQUARE (1 OUNCE) SEMISWEET CHOCOLATE, MELTED AND COOLED

SPECIAL EQUIPMENT

2 DECORATING BAGS

2 COUPLERS

2 WRITING TIPS (EACH ¼-INCH OPENING)

2 STAR TIPS (EACH ¼-INCH OPENING)

2 SMALL BASKETWEAVE TIPS (EACH ⅛-INCH OPENING)

1 Prepare Rich Chocolate Cupcakes as recipe directs, omitting the frosting.

2 Prepare White Chocolate Buttercream Frosting. Transfer 1½ cups frosting to a small bowl and set aside. To frosting remaining in larger bowl, beat in melted unsweetened and semisweet chocolates until blended. (You'll have slightly more chocolate frosting.) Spoon white frosting into decorating bag fitted with a coupler. Spoon chocolate frosting into another decorating bag fitted with another coupler.

3 Using white and semisweet chocolate frostings with suggested decorating tips, and small spatula, decorate tops of cupcakes as desired with black-and-white designs.

EACH CUPCAKE: ABOUT 290 CALORIES | 3G PROTEIN | 34G CARBOHYDRATE | 16G TOTAL FAT (8G SATURATED) | 0.5G FIBER | 66MG CHOLESTEROL | 193MG SODIUM

MILK CHOCOLATE CHEESECAKE

How to make classic cheesecake even creamier? Add milk chocolate with a dark cookie crust for kicks.

ACTIVE TIME: 25 MINUTES · **TOTAL TIME:** 1 HOUR 25 MINUTES PLUS COOLING AND CHILLING
MAKES: 16 SERVINGS

- 1 PACKAGE (9 OUNCES) CHOCOLATE WAFER COOKIES
- 6 TABLESPOONS BUTTER OR MARGARINE (¾ STICK), MELTED
- 2 PACKAGES (8 OUNCES EACH) CREAM CHEESE, SOFTENED
- ½ CUP PLUS 2 TABLESPOONS SUGAR
- ¼ TEASPOON SALT
- 3 LARGE EGGS, LIGHTLY BEATEN
- ¼ CUP WHOLE MILK
- 2 TEASPOONS VANILLA EXTRACT
- 1 BAG (11½ OUNCES) MILK CHOCOLATE CHIPS, MELTED
- 1½ CUPS SOUR CREAM

1 Preheat oven to 350°F. In food processor with knife blade attached, pulse chocolate cookies until fine crumbs form. Add butter to crumbs and pulse several times to combine. Transfer cookie mixture to 9-inch springform pan; press onto bottom and about 2 inches up side of pan to form crust. Bake crust 10 minutes. Cool completely in pan on wire rack.

2 In large bowl, with mixer on medium speed, beat cream cheese, ½ cup sugar, and salt 2 minutes or until smooth, occasionally scraping bowl with rubber spatula. Reduce speed to low. Add eggs, milk, and vanilla, and beat just until blended, occasionally scraping bowl. Add chocolate and beat until combined.

3 Pour cream-cheese mixture into crust. Bake cheesecake 45 minutes (it will jiggle slightly in center). Meanwhile, in small bowl, stir sour cream and remaining 2 tablespoons sugar until sugar dissolves; set aside.

4 Remove cheesecake from oven. Gently spread sour-cream mixture evenly on top. Return cheesecake to oven and bake 5 minutes longer to set sour cream.

5 Cool cheesecake completely in pan on wire rack. Cover and refrigerate at least 6 hours until well chilled, or up to 3 days before serving.

EACH SERVING: ABOUT 315 CALORIES | 5G PROTEIN | 27G CARBOHYDRATE | 22G TOTAL FAT (12G SATURATED) | 2G FIBER | 74MG CHOLESTEROL | 755MG SODIUM

TRIPLE-CHOCOLATE CHEESECAKE

Calling all chocoholics! Here's a triple-chocolate treat: chocolate wafers, semisweet chocolate, and cocoa.

ACTIVE TIME: 25 MINUTES · **TOTAL TIME:** 1 HOUR 25 MINUTES PLUS COOLING AND CHILLING
MAKES: 16 SERVINGS

1½ CUPS CHOCOLATE WAFER COOKIE CRUMBS

3 TABLESPOONS BUTTER OR MARGARINE, MELTED

2 TABLESPOONS PLUS 1 CUP SUGAR

3 PACKAGES (8 OUNCES EACH) CREAM CHEESE, SOFTENED

¼ CUP UNSWEETENED COCOA

4 LARGE EGGS

¾ CUP SOUR CREAM

1½ TEASPOONS VANILLA EXTRACT

8 SQUARES (8 OUNCES) SEMISWEET CHOCOLATE, MELTED AND COOLED

1 Preheat oven to 325°F. In 9" by 3" springform pan, combine cookie crumbs, melted butter, and 2 tablespoons sugar; stir with fork until evenly moistened. With hand, press mixture firmly onto bottom of pan. Bake 10 minutes. Cool completely in pan on wire rack.

2 In large bowl, with mixer at low speed, beat cream cheese until smooth. Beat in remaining 1 cup sugar and cocoa until blended, occasionally scraping bowl with rubber spatula. Reduce speed to low. Add eggs, one at a time, beating just until blended, scraping bowl. Beat in sour cream and vanilla. Add melted chocolate and beat until well blended.

3 Pour chocolate mixture over crust. Bake until cheesecake is set 2 inches from edge but center still jiggles, 50 to 55 minutes. Turn off oven; let cheesecake remain in oven with door ajar 1 hour. Remove from oven; run thin knife around edge of cheesecake to prevent cracking during cooling. Cool completely in pan on wire rack. Cover loosely and refrigerate until well chilled, at least 6 hours or up to overnight. Remove side of pan to serve.

EACH SERVING: ABOUT 384 CALORIES | 7G PROTEIN | 34G CARBOHYDRATE | 26G TOTAL FAT (15G SATURATED) | 2G FIBER | 111MG CHOLESTEROL | 237MG SODIUM

SILKEN CHOCOLATE CHEESECAKE

Silken tofu adds a wonderful, smooth texture to this lower-fat chocolate cheesecake. We dare you to stop at one forkful. (For photo, see page 6.)

ACTIVE TIME: 25 MINUTES · **TOTAL TIME:** 1 HOUR 15 MINUTES PLUS COOLING AND CHILLING

MAKES: 12 SERVINGS

---

1   CONTAINER (19 OUNCES) SILKEN TOFU

1   CONTAINER (15 OUNCES) PART-SKIM RICOTTA CHEESE

1   SQUARE (1 OUNCE) UNSWEETENED CHOCOLATE

1   PACKAGE (8 OUNCES) LIGHT CREAM CHEESE (NEUFCHÂTEL), SOFTENED

1   CUP PACKED DARK BROWN SUGAR

½   CUP UNSWEETENED COCOA

2   TEASPOONS VANILLA EXTRACT

FRESH STRAWBERRIES (OPTIONAL)

---

1   Preheat oven to 325°F. Line large sieve with two layers of paper towels and set over large bowl. Place tofu and ricotta in sieve and let stand 15 minutes to allow excess liquid to drain; discard liquid.

2   Transfer tofu mixture to food processor with knife blade attached; process until smooth.

3   In 1-quart saucepan, melt chocolate over low heat, stirring frequently, until smooth. Add ½ cup of tofu mixture to warm chocolate in pan; whisk until blended.

4   To tofu mixture remaining in food processor, add cream cheese, brown sugar, cocoa, vanilla, and chocolate mixture; process just until combined.

5   Pour mixture into 9" by 3" springform pan. Bake until cheesecake is set 2 inches from edge but center still jiggles, about 50 minutes. Cool cheesecake in pan on wire rack 1 hour. Cover loosely and refrigerate until well chilled, at least 6 hours or up to overnight.

6   To serve, remove side of pan; garnish with strawberries, if you like.

EACH SERVING: ABOUT 205 CALORIES | 9G PROTEIN | 25G CARBOHYDRATE | 9G TOTAL FAT (5G SATURATED) | 2G FIBER | 18MG CHOLESTEROL | 165MG SODIUM

RICH CHOCOLATE FROSTING

The combination of semisweet and unsweetened chocolates gives this frosting its perfect flavor balance.

ACTIVE TIME: 15 MINUTES

MAKES: 2½ CUPS

---

4   SQUARES (4 OUNCES) SEMISWEET CHOCOLATE

2   SQUARES (2 OUNCES) UNSWEETENED CHOCOLATE

2   CUPS CONFECTIONERS' SUGAR

¾   CUP BUTTER OR MARGARINE (1½ STICKS), SOFTENED

1   TEASPOON VANILLA EXTRACT

1   In heavy 1-quart saucepan, melt semisweet and unsweetened chocolates over low heat, stirring frequently, until smooth. Remove from heat; cool to room temperature.

2   In large bowl, with mixer at low speed, beat confectioners' sugar, butter, and vanilla until almost combined. Add melted chocolates. Increase speed to high; beat until light and fluffy, about 1 minute.

EACH TABLESPOON: ABOUT 75 CALORIES | 0G PROTEIN | 8G CARBOHYDRATE | 6G TOTAL FAT (3G SATURATED) | 0.5G FIBER | 9MG CHOLESTEROL | 36MG SODIUM

FIGURING FROSTING QUANTITIES

Here's how much frosting you'll need for the following cake sizes:

8-inch round, two layers	2¼ cups
8-inch round, three layers	2¾ cups
9-inch round, two layers	2⅔ cups
8-inch square, one layer	1⅓ cups
9-inch square, one layer	2 cups
13- by 9-inch, one layer	2⅓ cups
10-inch tube pan	2¼ cups
24 cupcakes	2¼ cups

CHOCOLATE BUTTER-CREAM FROSTING

This light, creamy frosting should be in every baker's repertoire.

ACTIVE TIME: 10 MINUTES

MAKES: 2¾ CUPS

---

2 CUPS CONFECTIONERS' SUGAR

1 CUP BUTTER OR MARGARINE
   (2 STICKS), SOFTENED

3 TABLESPOONS MILK

1 TEASPOON VANILLA EXTRACT

6 SQUARES (6 OUNCES) SEMISWEET
   CHOCOLATE, MELTED AND COOLED

In large bowl, with mixer at low speed, beat confectioners' sugar, butter, milk, vanilla, and cooled chocolate just until mixed. Increase speed to high; beat until light and fluffy, about 2 minutes, frequently scraping bowl with rubber spatula.

EACH TABLESPOON: ABOUT 80 CALORIES | 5G PROTEIN | 0G CARBOHYDRATE | 6G TOTAL FAT (3G SATURATED) | 0.5G FIBER | 3MG CHOLESTEROL | 51MG SODIUM

INTENSE CHOCOLATE BUTTER FROSTING

This frosting is super chocolatey, thanks to a one-two combo of cocoa powder and semisweet chocolate.

ACTIVE TIME: 15 MINUTES

MAKES: 2¾ CUPS

⅓ CUP UNSWEETENED COCOA

⅓ CUP BOILING WATER

1 CUP BUTTER OR MARGARINE (2 STICKS), SOFTENED

2 TABLESPOONS CONFECTIONERS' SUGAR

12 OUNCES SEMISWEET CHOCOLATE, MELTED AND COOLED

1 In small bowl, combine cocoa and boiling water, stirring until smooth.

2 In large bowl, with mixer at medium-high speed, beat butter and confectioner' sugar 5 minutes or until fluffy. Reduce speed to medium-low; add melted chocolate, then cocoa mixture, beating until smooth and occasionally scraping bowl with rubber spatula. If frosting is too runny, refrigerate until just stiff enough to spread.

EACH TABLESPOON: ABOUT 80 CALORIES | 1G PROTEIN | 5G CARBOHYDRATE | 7G TOTAL FAT (4G SATURATED) | 1G FIBER | 11MG CHOLESTEROL | 30MG SODIUM

FUDGE FROSTING

An extra-generous amount of chocolate makes this a frosting that any true chocolate lover will appreciate.

ACTIVE TIME: 15 MINUTES

MAKES: 2 CUPS

---

3 SQUARES (3 OUNCES) SEMISWEET CHOCOLATE

2 SQUARES (2 OUNCES) UNSWEETENED CHOCOLATE

½ CUP BUTTER OR MARGARINE (1 STICK), SOFTENED

1½ CUPS CONFECTIONERS' SUGAR

1½ TEASPOONS VANILLA EXTRACT

2 TO 3 TABLESPOONS MILK

---

1 In heavy 1-quart saucepan, melt semisweet and unsweetened chocolates over low heat, stirring frequently, until smooth. Remove from heat; cool slightly.

2 In large bowl, with mixer at low speed, beat melted chocolates and butter until blended. Add confectioners' sugar, vanilla, and 2 tablespoons milk; beat until smooth. Increase speed to medium-high; beat until frosting is light and fluffy, occasionally scraping bowl with rubber spatula. Beat in remaining 1 tablespoon milk as needed for easy spreading consistency.

EACH TABLESPOON: ABOUT 75 CALORIES | 1G PROTEIN | 8G CARBOHYDRATE | 5G TOTAL FAT (3G SATURATED) | 0.5G FIBER | 8MG CHOLESTEROL | 30MG SODIUM

SEMISWEET CHOCOLATE FROSTING

The combination of semisweet and unsweetened chocolates prevents the frosting from becoming overly sweet.

ACTIVE TIME: 15 MINUTES
MAKES: 2 CUPS

---

4 SQUARES (4 OUNCES) SEMISWEET CHOCOLATE

1 SQUARE (1 OUNCE) UNSWEETENED CHOCOLATE

½ CUP BUTTER (1 STICK), SOFTENED

1½ CUPS CONFECTIONERS' SUGAR

1½ TEASPOONS VANILLA EXTRACT

3 TO 4 TABLESPOONS MILK

1 In heavy 1-quart saucepan, melt semisweet and unsweetened chocolates over low heat, stirring frequently, until smooth. Cool slightly.

2 In large bowl, with mixer at low speed, beat melted chocolates and butter until blended. Add confectioners' sugar, vanilla, and 3 tablespoons milk; beat until smooth. Increase speed to medium-high; beat until light and fluffy, occasionally scraping bowl with rubber spatula. Beat in remaining 1 tablespoon milk as needed for easy spreading consistency.

EACH TABLESPOON: ABOUT 70 CALORIES | 0G PROTEIN | 8G CARBOHYDRATE | 5G TOTAL FAT (4G SATURATED) | 0.5G FIBER | 10MG CHOLESTEROL | 28MG SODIUM

MALTED-MILK FROSTING

Prepare Semisweet Chocolate Frosting as directed but beat in **2 tablespoons malted-milk powder** with confectioners' sugar in Step 2. Coarsely chop **½ cup malted-milk ball candies**; sprinkle over frosted cake.

EACH TABLESPOON: ABOUT 70 CALORIES | 0G PROTEIN | 8G CARBOHYDRATE | 4G TOTAL FAT (3G SATURATED) | 0.5G FIBER | 10MG CHOLESTEROL | 28MG SODIUM

MILK-CHOCOLATE FROSTING

Prepare Semisweet Chocolate Frosting as directed, but substitute **3 ounces milk chocolate**, melted and cooled, for semisweet chocolate.

EACH TABLESPOON: ABOUT 65 CALORIES | 0G PROTEIN | 8G CARBOHYDRATE | 4G TOTAL FAT (3G SATURATED) | 0.5G FIBER | 10MG CHOLESTEROL | 28MG SODIUM

MILK-CHOCOLATE CANDY BAR FROSTING

Subtle-tasting milk chocolate frosting is perfect for slathering over Devil's Food Cake (page 25) or our Checkerboard Cake (page 28).

ACTIVE TIME: 15 MINUTES

MAKES: 2¾ CUPS

¾ CUP BUTTER (1½ STICKS), SOFTENED

3 MILK-CHOCOLATE CANDY BARS (1½ TO 2 OUNCES EACH), MELTED AND COOLED

1½ CUPS CONFECTIONERS' SUGAR

3 TO 4 TABLESPOONS MILK

In large bowl, with mixer at low speed, beat softened butter and melted chocolate until blended. Add confectioners' sugar and 3 tablespoons milk. Beat until smooth, adding remaining 1 tablespoon milk as needed for easy spreading consistency. Increase speed to medium-high; beat until fluffy, about 1 minute.

EACH TABLESPOON: ABOUT 70 CALORIES | 0G PROTEIN | 6G CARBOHYDRATE | 5G TOTAL FAT (4G SATURATED) | 0G FIBER | 12MG CHOLESTEROL | 45MG SODIUM

WHITE CHOCOLATE BUTTERCREAM FROSTING

This scrumptious buttery, creamy frosting will make any cake—plain or fancy—special.

ACTIVE TIME: 15 MINUTES

MAKES: 3½ CUPS

---

1 CUP BUTTER (2 STICKS), SOFTENED

2½ CUPS CONFECTIONERS' SUGAR

6 OUNCES WHITE CHOCOLATE, SWISS CONFECTIONERY BARS, OR WHITE BAKING BAR, MELTED BUT STILL WARM

¼ CUP MILK

1½ TEASPOONS VANILLA EXTRACT

In large bowl, with mixer at high speed, beat butter, confectioners' sugar, white chocolate, milk, and vanilla until just mixed. Increase speed to high; beat until light and fluffy, about 2 minutes.

EACH TABLESPOON: ABOUT 65 CALORIES | 0G PROTEIN | 7G CARBOHYDRATE | 4G TOTAL FAT (3G SATURATED) | 0G FIBER | 9MG CHOLESTEROL | 39MG SODIUM

COLORING FROSTING

For tinting frosting and icings, the pros prefer paste food colors (also called icing colors), which do not dilute the frosting as liquid colors can. Add paste coloring a tiny bit at a time, using the tip of a toothpick: The colors are extremely intense.

TWO-TONE BRANDIED BUTTER FROSTING

Just a touch of brandy (or cognac) adds elegance to this silky smooth frosting. If you like the combination of chocolate and fruit, substitute raspberry- or orange-flavored liqueur.

ACTIVE TIME: 15 MINUTES · **TOTAL TIME:** 25 MINUTES PLUS COOLING
MAKES: 1½ CUPS OF EACH FLAVOR

1   CUP SUGAR

½   CUP ALL-PURPOSE FLOUR

1   CUP MILK

1   SQUARE (1 OUNCE) SEMISWEET CHOCOLATE

1   SQUARE (1 OUNCE) UNSWEETENED CHOCOLATE

1   CUP BUTTER OR MARGARINE (2 STICKS), SOFTENED

2   TABLESPOONS BRANDY

1   TEASPOON VANILLA EXTRACT

1   In 2-quart saucepan, combine sugar and flour. With wire whisk, mix in milk until smooth. Cook over medium-high heat, stirring often, until mixture thickens and boils. Reduce heat to low; cook, stirring constantly, 2 minutes. Remove from heat; cool completely.

2   Meanwhile, in heavy 1-quart saucepan, melt semisweet and unsweetened chocolates over low heat, stirring frequently, until smooth. Remove from heat; cool slightly.

3   In large bowl, with mixer at medium speed, beat butter until creamy. Gradually beat in cooled milk mixture. When mixture is smooth, beat in brandy and vanilla until blended. Spoon half of vanilla frosting into small bowl; stir cooled chocolate into remaining frosting in larger bowl.

EACH TABLESPOON VANILLA FROSTING: ABOUT 60 CALORIES | 0G PROTEIN
5G CARBOHYDRATE | 4G TOTAL FAT (2G SATURATED) | 0G FIBER | 11MG CHOLESTEROL
40MG SODIUM

EACH TABLESPOON CHOCOLATE FROSTING: ABOUT 70 CALORIES | 0G PROTEIN
6G CARBOHYDRATE | 5G TOTAL FAT (3G SATURATED) | 0.5G FIBER | 11MG CHOLESTEROL
40MG SODIUM

COCONUT-PECAN FROSTING

This unique cooked frosting is an absolute must for German's Chocolate Cake (page 26); you can also spread it on any chocolate or vanilla layer or sheet cake.

ACTIVE TIME: 5 MINUTES · **TOTAL TIME:** 20 MINUTES

MAKES: 3 CUPS

½ CUP BUTTER OR MARGARINE (1 STICK), CUT INTO PIECES

1 CUP HEAVY OR WHIPPING CREAM

1 CUP PACKED LIGHT BROWN SUGAR

3 LARGE EGG YOLKS

1 TEASPOON VANILLA EXTRACT

1 CUP FLAKED SWEETENED COCONUT

1 CUP PECANS (4 OUNCES), CHOPPED

1 In 2-quart saucepan, combine butter, cream, and brown sugar. Heat almost to boiling over medium-high heat, stirring occasionally.

2 Place egg yolks in medium bowl. Slowly pour about ½ cup hot sugar mixture into egg yolks, whisking constantly. Reduce heat to medium-low. Add egg-yolk mixture to saucepan; whisk until mixture has thickened (do not boil). Remove from heat. Stir in vanilla, coconut, and pecans until combined. Cool to room temperature.

EACH TABLESPOON: ABOUT 80 CALORIES │ 1G PROTEIN │ 6G CARBOHYDRATE │ 6G TOTAL FAT (3G SATURATED) │ 0G FIBER │ 25MG CHOLESTEROL │ 30MG SODIUM

PEANUT BUTTER FROSTING

Here's a quick fix for chocolate and peanut butter lovers: Lavish One-Bowl Chocolate Cake (page 19) with this creamy Peanut Butter Frosting.

ACTIVE TIME: 10 MINUTES
MAKES: 2¾ CUPS

½ CUP BUTTER OR MARGARINE (1 STICK), SOFTENED

½ CUP CREAMY PEANUT BUTTER

1 SMALL PACKAGE (3 OUNCES) CREAM CHEESE, SOFTENED

1 TEASPOON VANILLA EXTRACT

2 CUPS CONFECTIONERS' SUGAR

2 TO 3 TABLESPOONS MILK

1 In large bowl, with mixer at medium speed, beat butter, peanut butter, cream cheese, and vanilla until smooth and fluffy.

2 Add confectioners' sugar and 2 tablespoons milk; beat until blended. Increase speed to medium-high; beat until fluffy, about 2 minutes, adding remaining 1 tablespoon milk as needed for desired spreading consistency.

EACH TABLESPOON: ABOUT 65 CALORIES | 1G PROTEIN | 6G CARBOHYDRATE | 4G TOTAL FAT (2G SATURATED) | 0G FIBER | 8MG CHOLESTEROL | 40MG SODIUM

FLUFFY WHITE FROSTING

This marshmallowlike frosting is best enjoyed the day it is made. If you're planning on frosting a chocolate cake, omit the lemon juice.

ACTIVE TIME: 15 MINUTES · **TOTAL TIME:** 20 MINUTES
MAKES: 3 CUPS

2   LARGE EGG WHITES

1   CUP SUGAR

¼   CUP WATER

2   TEASPOONS FRESH LEMON JUICE
    (OPTIONAL)

1   TEASPOON LIGHT CORN SYRUP

¼   TEASPOON CREAM OF TARTAR

1 Set medium bowl over 3- to 4-quart saucepan filled with 1 inch simmering water (bowl should sit about 2 inches above water). With hand-held mixer at high speed, beat egg whites, sugar, water, lemon juice if using, corn syrup, and cream of tartar in bowl. Beat until soft peaks form when beaters are lifted and mixture reaches 160°F on candy thermometer, about 7 minutes.

2 Remove bowl from pan; beat egg-white mixture until stiff, glossy peaks form when beaters are lifted, 5 to 10 minutes longer.

EACH TABLESPOON: ABOUT 17 CALORIES | 0G PROTEIN | 4G CARBOHYDRATE | 0G TOTAL FAT (0G SATURATED) | 0G FIBER | 0MG CHOLESTEROL | 2MG SODIUM

WHIPPED CREAM FROSTING

For the times when a cake needs no more embellishment than some freshly whipped cream.

ACTIVE TIME: 5 MINUTES

MAKES: 4 CUPS

---

2   CUPS HEAVY OR WHIPPING CREAM

¼   CUP CONFECTIONERS' SUGAR

1   TEASPOON VANILLA EXTRACT

In small bowl, with mixer at medium speed, beat cream, confectioners' sugar, and vanilla until stiff peaks form.

EACH TABLESPOON: ABOUT 28 CALORIES | 0G PROTEIN | 2G CARBOHYDRATE | 3G TOTAL FAT (2G SATURATED) | 0G FIBER | 10MG CHOLESTEROL | 3MG SODIUM

COCOA WHIPPED CREAM FROSTING

Prepare as directed but use **½ cup confectioners' sugar** and add **½ cup unsweetened cocoa**.

EACH TABLESPOON: ABOUT 30 CALORIES | 0G PROTEIN | 2G CARBOHYDRATE | 3G TOTAL FAT (2G SATURATED) | 0G FIBER | 10MG CHOLESTEROL | 3MG SODIUM

COFFEE WHIPPED CREAM FROSTING

Prepare as for Whipped Cream Frosting but dissolve **2 teaspoons instant coffee powder** in **2 teaspoons hot water**; cool. Beat into whipped cream.

EACH TABLESPOON: ABOUT 30 CALORIES | 0G PROTEIN | 1G CARBOHYDRATE | 3G TOTAL FAT (2G SATURATED) | 0G FIBER | 10MG CHOLESTEROL | 5MG SODIUM

CHOCOLATE GLAZE

Pour or spread the warm (not hot) glaze over Chocolate Éclairs (page 148). The glaze will thicken and set as it cools.

ACTIVE TIME: 5 MINUTES · **TOTAL TIME:** 10 MINUTES

MAKES: ½ CUP

---

3   SQUARES (3 OUNCES) SEMISWEET CHOCOLATE, COARSELY CHOPPED

3   TABLESPOONS BUTTER

1   TABLESPOON LIGHT CORN SYRUP

1   TABLESPOON MILK

In heavy 1-quart saucepan, heat chocolate, butter, corn syrup, and milk over low heat, stirring occasionally, until smooth.

EACH TABLESPOON: ABOUT 100 CALORIES | 1G PROTEIN | 9G CARBOHYDRATE | 8G TOTAL FAT (5G SATURATED) | 1G FIBER | 12MG CHOLESTEROL | 50MG SODIUM

MOCHA GLAZE

Pour or spread the warm (not hot) glaze over Chocolate Éclairs (page 148). The glaze will thicken and set as it cools.

TOTAL TIME: 5 MINUTES

MAKES: 1 CUP

¼ TEASPOON INSTANT ESPRESSO-COFFEE POWDER

2 TABLESPOONS HOT WATER

3 TABLESPOONS UNSWEETENED COCOA

3 TABLESPOONS DARK CORN SYRUP

1 TABLESPOON COFFEE-FLAVORED LIQUEUR

1 CUP CONFECTIONERS' SUGAR

In medium bowl, dissolve coffee powder in hot water. Stir in cocoa, corn syrup, and liqueur until blended. Stir in confectioners' sugar until smooth.

EACH TABLESPOON: ABOUT 45 CALORIES | 0G PROTEIN | 11G CARBOHYDRATE | 0G TOTAL FAT (0G SATURATED) | 0.5G FIBER | 0MG CHOLESTEROL | 5MG SODIUM

GANACHE

Ganache is the richest of all chocolate frosting—virtually a spreadable fudge. It's the chocolate selection that will make or break this recipe, so choose a fine-quality semisweet. If the ganache is too thick to spread when you take it out of the refrigerator, let it stand at room temperature until softened.

TOTAL TIME: 15 MINUTES PLUS CHILLING

MAKES: 2 CUPS

1 CUP HEAVY OR WHIPPING CREAM	1 TEASPOON VANILLA EXTRACT
2 TABLESPOONS SUGAR	1 TO 2 TABLESPOONS BRANDY OR
2 TEASPOONS BUTTER OR MARGARINE	ORANGE- OR ALMOND-FLAVORED LIQUEUR (OPTIONAL)
10 SQUARES (10 OUNCES) SEMISWEET CHOCOLATE, CHOPPED	

1 In 2-quart saucepan, combine cream, sugar, and butter; heat to boiling over medium-high heat. Remove from heat.

2 Add chocolate to cream mixture; with wire whisk stir until chocolate melts and mixture is smooth. Stir in vanilla and, if using, brandy. Pour into jelly-roll pan and refrigerate until spreadable, at least 30 minutes.

EACH TABLESPOON: ABOUT 75 CALORIES | 1G PROTEIN | 6G CARBOHYDRATE | 6G TOTAL FAT (3G SATURATED) | 1G FIBER | 11MG CHOLESTEROL | 6MG SODIUM

PIES & TARTS

A pie or tart is only as good as its crust, so here's how to bake the best. The flavor and texture of a crust depends on its main ingredients: flour and fat. Butter gives dough flavor, crispness, and color; vegetable shortening makes it flaky. We like to use a combination of butter and shortening.

MIX IT RIGHT A pastry blender is the best tool for blending fat and flour. Work quickly so the fat remains firm. Then sprinkle in the water, 1 tablespoon at a time, tossing with a fork after each addition. When enough water has been added, the dough will no longer look dusty. Shape it into one or more disks. Wrap in plastic and chill for at least 30 minutes, so it has a chance to firm up and the water can distribute itself throughout the dough.

ROLL IT OUT Lightly dust the surface (and rolling pin) with flour. To roll the dough into a round, start in the center and roll up to the edge. Give the dough a quarter turn; repeat rolling and rotating until you have a round.

A PERFECT FIT We like to use glass or dull metal pie plates. To transfer dough to a pie plate or tart pan; loosely roll the dough onto the rolling pin. Position the pin at one side of the pie plate and unroll the dough. Or fold the dough into quarters, set it into the pan, and unfold. Gently press the dough against the bottom and side of the pan (do not stretch it).

MAKE IT PRETTY You can use your fingertips to crimp and shape a rope or scalloped edge, use a fork to make an old-fashioned forked edge, or use a knife to make slits around the edge at about ¼-inch intervals and fold over every other piece to form a turret edge. If you have more time, use a cookie cutter to cut out decorative shapes, such as hearts or leaves, and attach them to the plain edge with water or beaten egg white.

Chocolate-Cream Meringue Pie (page 79)

BLACK-BOTTOM PIE

Deserving of its classic status, this pie is both rich and light; it is layered with rum and chocolate custards and topped with cream.

ACTIVE TIME: 40 MINUTES · **TOTAL TIME:** 50 MINUTES PLUS COOLING AND CHILLING
MAKES: 10 SERVINGS

CHOCOLATE WAFER CRUMB CRUST
(PAGE 100) OR COCONUT PASTRY
CRUST (PAGE 101)

1   TEASPOON UNFLAVORED GELATIN

2   TABLESPOONS COLD WATER

1½ CUPS MILK

¾   CUP SUGAR

4   LARGE EGG YOLKS

2   SQUARES (2 OUNCES) UNSWEETENED
CHOCOLATE, MELTED

½   TEASPOON VANILLA EXTRACT

2   TEASPOONS DARK RUM OR 1
TEASPOON VANILLA EXTRACT

2   CUPS HEAVY OR WHIPPING CREAM

1   Prepare crust as directed. Cool completely.

2   In cup, evenly sprinkle gelatin over cold water; let stand 2 minutes to soften gelatin slightly.

3   Meanwhile, in 2-quart saucepan, combine milk and ½ cup sugar; cook over medium heat, stirring, until bubbles form around edge.

4   In small bowl, with wire whisk, lightly beat egg yolks. Beat about ⅓ cup hot milk mixture into egg yolks. Slowly pour egg-yolk mixture back into milk mixture, whisking rapidly to prevent curdling. Cook over low heat, stirring constantly, until mixture has thickened slightly and coats back of spoon, about 10 minutes. (Temperature on thermometer should reach about 160°F; do not boil, or mixture will curdle.)

5   Transfer 1 cup milk mixture to small bowl. Stir in melted chocolate and vanilla until blended. Pour into cooled crust; refrigerate.

6   Over low heat, add softened gelatin to remaining milk mixture in saucepan; stir until gelatin has completely dissolved. Remove from heat. Stir in rum. Cool to room temperature, stirring occasionally.

7   In bowl, with mixer, beat cream with remaining ¼ cup sugar until stiff peaks form. Whisk half of whipped cream into cooled gelatin mixture. Refrigerate remaining whipped cream. Spoon gelatin-cream mixture over chocolate layer. Cover; refrigerate until firm, about 3 hours. To serve, mound remaining whipped cream over filling.

EACH SERVING: ABOUT 410 CALORIES | 5G PROTEIN | 31G CARBOHYDRATE | 31G TOTAL FAT
(18G SATURATED) | 1G FIBER | 168MG CHOLESTEROL | 171MG SODIUM

CHOCOLATE-CREAM MERINGUE PIE

This time-tested favorite is made with whipped chocolate cream nestled in a meringue crust. Heavenly!

ACTIVE TIME: 30 MINUTES · **TOTAL TIME:** 1 HOUR 30 MINUTES PLUS COOLING
MAKES: 10 SERVINGS

3   LARGE EGG WHITES

¼   TEASPOON CREAM OF TARTAR

¼   TEASPOON SALT

2¼ CUPS CONFECTIONERS' SUGAR

2½ TEASPOONS VANILLA EXTRACT

½   CUP UNSWEETENED COCOA

1   TEASPOON INSTANT ESPRESSO-COFFEE POWDER

1   TEASPOON HOT WATER

2   TABLESPOONS MILK

2   CUPS HEAVY OR WHIPPING CREAM

CHOCOLATE CURLS (PAGE 166)

1 Preheat oven to 300°F. Line 9-inch pie plate with foil, extending foil over rim of plate. Press foil against pie plate; grease and flour foil.

2 In small bowl, with mixer at high speed, beat egg whites, cream of tartar, and salt until soft peaks form when beaters are lifted. Sprinkle in 1 cup confectioners' sugar, 2 tablespoons at a time, beating until sugar has dissolved. Add 1 teaspoon vanilla; continue beating until egg whites stand in stiff, glossy peaks when beaters are lifted.

3 With large spoon, spread meringue evenly over bottom and up side of pie plate, extending meringue ½ inch above rim of pie plate. Bake 1 hour. Turn off oven and let meringue remain in oven 1 hour to dry. Cool meringue shell completely in pie plate on wire rack. Lift shell from pie plate and peel off foil. Place shell on serving plate.

4 Meanwhile, prepare filling: Sift cocoa with remaining 1¼ cups confectioners' sugar. In cup, dissolve espresso powder in hot water; stir in milk. In large bowl, with mixer at medium speed, beat cream, espresso, and remaining 1½ teaspoons vanilla until soft peaks form. Reduce speed to low; gradually beat in cocoa mixture until thoroughly blended and stiff peaks form.

5 With rubber spatula, spread chocolate cream in cooled meringue shell. If not serving right away, cover pie and refrigerate until ready to serve, up to 4 hours. Sprinkle with chocolate curls.

EACH SERVING: ABOUT 290 CALORIES | 3G PROTEIN | 31G CARBOHYDRATE | 18G TOTAL FAT (11G SATURATED) | 1G FIBER | 66MG CHOLESTEROL | 95MG SODIUM

FAVORITE CHOCOLATE CREAM PIE

Cream pies, as we know them today, have been popular in America for the last hundred years or so. If you prefer the piecrust to remain on the crisp side, serve the pie fairly soon after the filling has firmed up.

ACTIVE TIME: 35 MINUTES · **TOTAL TIME:** 40 MINUTES PLUS COOLING AND CHILLING
MAKES: 10 SERVINGS

CHOCOLATE WAFER CRUMB CRUST (PAGE 100)

¾ CUP SUGAR

1/3 CUP CORNSTARCH

½ TEASPOON SALT

3¾ CUPS MILK

5 LARGE EGG YOLKS

3 SQUARES (3 OUNCES) UNSWEETENED CHOCOLATE, MELTED

2 TABLESPOONS BUTTER OR MARGARINE, CUT INTO PIECES

2 TEASPOONS VANILLA EXTRACT

CHOCOLATE CURLS (PAGE 166, OPTIONAL)

1 CUP HEAVY OR WHIPPING CREAM

1 Prepare crust as directed. Cool.

2 Meanwhile, in heavy 3-quart saucepan, combine sugar, cornstarch, and salt; with wire whisk, stir in milk until smooth. Cook over medium heat, stirring constantly, until mixture has thickened and boils; boil 1 minute. In small bowl, with wire whisk, lightly beat egg yolks. Beat ½ cup hot milk mixture into beaten egg yolks. Slowly pour egg-yolk mixture back into milk mixture, stirring rapidly to prevent curdling. Cook over low heat, stirring constantly, until mixture is very thick or temperature on thermometer reaches 160°F.

3 Remove saucepan from heat; stir in chocolate, butter, and vanilla until butter has melted and mixture is smooth. Pour hot chocolate filling into cooled crust; press plastic wrap onto surface. Refrigerate until filling is set, about 4 hours.

4 Meanwhile, make chocolate curls, if using.

5 To serve, in small bowl, with mixer at medium speed, beat cream until stiff peaks form; spoon over chocolate filling. Top with chocolate curls, if desired.

EACH SERVING: ABOUT 415 CALORIES | 7G PROTEIN | 38G CARBOHYDRATE | 28G TOTAL FAT (16G SATURATED) | 2G FIBER | 171MG CHOLESTEROL | 329G SODIUM

FUDGE PECAN PIE

Serve this dense brownie-like pie with a generous bowl of softly whipped, bourbon-spiked cream.

ACTIVE TIME: 30 MINUTES · **TOTAL TIME:** 1 HOUR 35 MINUTES PLUS COOLING
MAKES: 10 SERVINGS

PASTRY

1½ CUPS ALL-PURPOSE FLOUR

½ TEASPOON SALT

4 TABLESPOONS COLD BUTTER OR MARGARINE

¼ CUP VEGETABLE SHORTENING

3 TO 5 TABLESPOONS ICE WATER

FILLING

4 TABLESPOONS BUTTER OR MARGARINE

2 SQUARES (2 OUNCES) UNSWEETENED CHOCOLATE

1 BOTTLE (16 OUNCES) LIGHT CORN SYRUP

4 LARGE EGGS

1 TEASPOON VANILLA EXTRACT

¼ CUP ALL-PURPOSE FLOUR

¼ CUP SUGAR

¼ TEASPOON SALT

1½ CUPS PECAN HALVES

1 Prepare Pastry: In large bowl, combine flour and salt. With pastry blender or two knives used scissor-fashion, cut in butter and shortening until mixture resembles coarse crumbs.

2 Sprinkle in ice water, 1 tablespoon at a time, mixing lightly with fork after each addition, until dough is just moist enough to hold together. Shape dough into disk; wrap in plastic wrap. Refrigerate 30 minutes or up to overnight. If chilled overnight, let stand 30 minutes at room temperature before rolling.

3 Meanwhile, prepare Filling: In 4-quart saucepan, melt butter and chocolate over low heat, stirring frequently, until smooth. With wire whisk, mix in corn syrup, eggs, and vanilla. Gradually whisk in flour, sugar, and salt until blended.

4 Preheat oven to 350°F. On lightly floured surface, with floured rolling pin, roll dough into 13-inch round. Gently roll dough round onto rolling pin and ease into 9½-inch deep-dish pie plate, gently pressing dough against side of plate. Trim edge, leaving 1-inch overhang. Fold overhang under; form high decorative edge (opposite).

5 Chop 1 cup pecans; sprinkle over crust. Carefully pour chocolate mixture over pecans. Arrange remaining ½ cup pecan halves on top. Bake until filling is set and knife inserted 1 inch from edge comes out almost clean, 65 to 75 minutes. Cool on wire rack.

EACH SERVING: ABOUT 520 CALORIES | 7G PROTEIN | 59G CARBOHYDRATE | 30G TOTAL FAT (8G SATURATED) | 3G FIBER | 95MG CHOLESTEROL | 328MG SODIUM

TWO DECORATIVE PIE EDGES

A classic border is the perfect way to add a professional finish to homemade pies.

To make a crimped edge: With kitchen shears, trim the dough edge, leaving a 1-inch overhang. Fold the overhang under; form a stand-up edge. Push one index finger against the inside edge of the rim; with the index finger and thumb of the other hand, pinch dough to flute. Repeat all around.

To make a rope edge: With kitchen shears, trim the dough edge, leaving a 1-inch overhang. Fold the overhang under; form a stand-up edge. Press thumb into dough edge at an angle, then pinch dough between thumb and knuckle of index finger. Place thumb in groove left by index finger; pinch as before. Repeat all around.

GEORGIA CHOCOLATE-PECAN PIE

This sinfully rich creation will be a favorite with any chocolate lover.

ACTIVE TIME: 45 MINUTES · **TOTAL TIME:** 1 HOUR 50 MINUTES PLUS COOLING
MAKES: 12 SERVINGS

PASTRY DOUGH FOR 1-CRUST PIE (PAGE 98)

4 TABLESPOONS BUTTER OR MARGARINE

2 SQUARES (2 OUNCES) UNSWEETENED CHOCOLATE

1¾ CUPS PECAN HALVES (7 OUNCES)

¾ CUP PACKED DARK BROWN SUGAR

¾ CUP DARK CORN SYRUP

1 TEASPOON VANILLA EXTRACT

3 LARGE EGGS

1 Prepare dough as directed through chilling.

2 On lightly floured surface, with floured rolling pin, roll dough into 12-inch round. Gently roll dough round onto rolling pin and ease into 9-inch pie plate, gently pressing dough against side of plate. Trim edge, leaving 1-inch overhang. Fold overhang under; make decorative edge (page 83). Refrigerate or freeze until firm, 10 to 15 minutes.

3 Preheat oven to 425°F. In heavy 1-quart saucepan, melt butter and chocolate over low heat, stirring frequently, until smooth. Cool slightly.

4 Line pie shell with foil; fill with pie weights or dry beans. Bake 15 minutes. Remove foil with weights; bake until golden, 5 to 10 minutes longer. If shell puffs up during baking, gently press it down with back of spoon. Cool on wire rack. Turn oven control to 350°F.

5 Coarsely chop 1 cup pecans. In large bowl, with wire whisk, mix cooled chocolate mixture, brown sugar, corn syrup, vanilla, and eggs until blended. Stir in chopped pecans and remaining pecan halves.

6 Pour pecan mixture into cooled pie shell. Bake until filling is set around edges but center jiggles slightly, 45 to 50 minutes. Cool on wire rack at least 1 hour for easier slicing.

EACH SERVING: ABOUT 395 CALORIES | 5G PROTEIN | 43G CARBOHYDRATE | 24G TOTAL FAT (4G SATURATED) | 3G FIBER | 53MG CHOLESTEROL | 225MG SODIUM

CHOCOLATE-WALNUT PIE

Imagine an ultrarich, walnutty fudge brownie baked in a shortbread crust. Sound good? Here's the recipe. All you have to decide is whether to serve it warm or cool, and whether to add a big spoonful of whipped cream or a scoop of vanilla or coffee ice cream.

ACTIVE TIME: 30 MINUTES · **TOTAL TIME:** 1 HOUR PLUS COOLING
MAKES: 12 SERVINGS

SHORTBREAD CRUST (PAGE 99)

½ CUP BUTTER OR MARGARINE (1 STICK)

3 SQUARES (3 OUNCES) UNSWEETENED CHOCOLATE

½ CUP PACKED LIGHT BROWN SUGAR

½ CUP GRANULATED SUGAR

2 LARGE EGGS

¾ CUP ALL-PURPOSE FLOUR

⅛ TEASPOON SALT

1 TEASPOON VANILLA EXTRACT

¾ CUP WALNUTS, COARSELY CHOPPED

1 Prepare crust as directed.

2 Preheat oven to 325°F. In 3-quart saucepan, melt butter and chocolate over low heat, stirring frequently, until smooth. Remove from heat and stir in brown and granulated sugars until blended. Add eggs, one at a time, stirring well after each addition. Stir in flour, salt, vanilla, and walnuts until well blended. Pour into cooled baked piecrust.

3 Bake until top is just set, about 30 minutes. Cool on wire rack 1 hour to serve warm, or cool completely to serve later.

EACH SERVING: ABOUT 385 CALORIES | 5G PROTEIN | 39G CARBOHYDRATE | 25G TOTAL FAT (13G SATURATED) | 2G FIBER | 77MG CHOLESTEROL | 195MG SODIUM

DARK CHOCOLATE–WALNUT CARAMEL PIE

This decadent pie, made with dark chocolate, creamy homemade caramel, and toasted walnuts, is well worth the calorie splurge.

ACTIVE TIME: 25 MINUTES · **TOTAL TIME:** 45 MINUTES PLUS CHILLING AND COOLING
MAKES: 12 SERVINGS

PASTRY DOUGH FOR 1-CRUST PIE (SEE PAGE 98)

1 CUP SUGAR

¼ CUP WATER

1¼ CUPS HEAVY OR WHIPPING CREAM

8 SQUARES (8 OUNCES) SEMISWEET CHOCOLATE, CUT UP

2 TABLESPOONS BUTTER OR MARGARINE

2 TEASPOONS VANILLA EXTRACT

1¾ CUPS WALNUTS, TOASTED AND COARSELY CHOPPED

1 Prepare dough as recipe directs. On lightly floured surface, with floured rolling pin, roll dough into 12-inch round. Gently roll round onto pin and ease into 9-inch pie plate, gently pressing dough against side. Trim edge, leaving 1-inch overhang. Fold overhang under and make decorative edge (page 83). Refrigerate or freeze until firm, 10 to 15 minutes.

2 Bake crust as directed but increase baking time after removing pie weights by 2 minutes or until deep golden. Cool pie shell on wire rack at least 15 minutes.

3 In 3-quart saucepan, heat sugar and water on medium-high until sugar dissolves and turns amber, 15 minutes, swirling pan occasionally.

4 Meanwhile, in microwave-safe cup, heat ¾ cup cream in microwave on High 45 seconds or until warm. Keep remaining cream cold.

5 Remove saucepan from heat. Stir in warm cream until a smooth caramel forms (caramel will stiffen when cream is added). Stir in chocolate and butter until melted. Stir in vanilla and 1½ cups walnuts.

6 Pour warm chocolate filling into pie shell. Cool 1 hour on wire rack, then cover and refrigerate at least 3 hours or until set.

7 When ready to serve, in medium bowl, with mixer on medium speed, beat remaining ½ cup cream until soft peaks form. With metal spatula, spread whipped cream on top of pie, leaving ½-inch border. Sprinkle with remaining walnuts.

EACH SERVING: ABOUT 500 CALORIES | 6G PROTEIN | 40G CARBOHYDRATE | 37G TOTAL FAT (15G SATURATED) | 3G FIBER | 53MG CHOLESTEROL | 130MG SODIUM

CHOCOLATE PUDDING PIE WITH COCONUT CRUST

A velvety-smooth homemade chocolate pudding in a toasted-coconut crust—topped with luscious whipped cream. Impossible to resist!

TOTAL TIME: 40 MINUTES PLUS CHILLING
MAKES: 10 SERVINGS

COCONUT PASTRY CRUST (PAGE 101)

¾ CUP SUGAR

⅓ CUP CORNSTARCH

½ TEASPOON SALT

3¾ CUPS MILK

5 LARGE EGG YOLKS

3 SQUARES (3 OUNCES) UNSWEETENED CHOCOLATE, MELTED

2 TEASPOONS VANILLA EXTRACT

2 TABLESPOONS BUTTER OR MARGARINE

1 CUP HEAVY OR WHIPPING CREAM

¼ CUP FLAKED SWEETENED COCONUT, TOASTED

1 Prepare crust, bake, and cool as directed.

2 In 3-quart saucepan, stir together sugar, cornstarch, and salt; stir in milk until smooth. Cook, stirring constantly, over medium heat until mixture is thickened and boils; boil 1 minute. In small bowl, with wire whisk or fork, beat egg yolks lightly. Beat small amount of hot milk mixture into yolk mixture. Slowly pour yolk mixture back into milk mixture, stirring rapidly to prevent lumping. Cook over low heat 2 minutes, stirring constantly, until very thick, or an instant-read thermometer registers 160°F when placed in custard.

3 Remove saucepan from heat and stir in melted chocolate, vanilla, and butter; blend well. Pour filling into cooled piecrust. Place plastic wrap on surface of filling. Refrigerate 4 hours, or until filling is set.

4 In chilled bowl, with mixer at medium speed, whip cream until stiff peaks form. Pipe or spoon whipped cream over filling. Sprinkle toasted coconut on top.

EACH SERVING: ABOUT 455 CALORIES | 7G PROTEIN | 41G CARBOHYDRATE | 31G TOTAL FAT (18G SATURATED) | 2G FIBER | 177MG CHOLESTEROL | 285MG SODIUM

SWISS CHOCOLATE ALMOND TART

What's not to like about a chocolate almond crust topped with a delectable chocolate and cream cheese filling sprinkled with almonds?

ACTIVE TIME: 15 MINUTES · **TOTAL TIME:** 55 MINUTES PLUS COOLING AND CHILLING
MAKES: 12 SERVINGS

½ CUPS SLIVERED ALMONDS

1¼ CUPS CHOCOLATE-COOKIE CRUMBS

6 TABLESPOONS (¾ STICK) BUTTER OR MARGARINE, MELTED

6 OUNCES WHITE CHOCOLATE, CHOPPED

1 PACKAGE (8 OUNCES) CREAM CHEESE, SOFTENED

½ TEASPOON VANILLA EXTRACT

1½ CUPS HEAVY CREAM, SUBSTITUTE WHIPPING CREAM

6 SQUARES (6 OUNCES) SEMISWEET CHOCOLATE, CHOPPED

2 TABLESPOONS CHOCOLATE-FLAVORED LIQUEUR (OPTIONAL)

1 Preheat oven to 350°F. Place almonds in 8-inch square metal baking pan. Bake almonds 12 to 15 minutes until golden, stirring occasionally; let cool.

2 In food processor with knife blade attached or in blender at medium speed, blend half the almonds until finely ground. Set aside remaining almonds for garnish. In medium bowl, with fork, combine ground almonds with cookie crumbs and butter.

3 Spoon crumb mixture into ungreased 9-inch tart pan with removable bottom; press evenly onto bottom and up side of tart pan. Bake crust 15 minutes; cool completely in pan on wire rack.

4 In heavy 1-quart saucepan over low heat, heat white chocolate, cream cheese, vanilla, and ¾ cup cream, whisking constantly, until mixture is smooth, about 10 minutes. Pour into crust; spread to make an even layer. Refrigerate tart, uncovered, 1 hour. Wash and dry saucepan.

5 Place semisweet chocolate in small bowl. In same saucepan over medium-low heat, heat liqueur, if using, and remaining ¾ cup cream just to boiling. Pour cream mixture over chocolate; let stand 30 seconds; gently stir until smooth.

6 Pour chocolate mixture into crust over white layer, spreading evenly with small metal spatula. Refrigerate tart overnight.

7 To serve, remove side of tart pan; place tart on dessert platter. Sprinkle reserved almonds around edge of tart.

EACH SERVING: ABOUT 445 CALORIES | 5G PROTEIN | 27G CARBOHYDRATE | 36G TOTAL FAT (18G SATURATED FAT) | 2G FIBER | 65MG CHOLESTEROL | 200MG SODIUM

CHOCOLATE TRUFFLE TART

So unbelievably decadent, one thin slice is all you'll need.

ACTIVE TIME: 20 MINUTES · **TOTAL TIME:** 1 HOUR PLUS CHILLING AND COOLING
MAKES: 12 SERVINGS

TART PASTRY

1   CUP ALL-PURPOSE FLOUR

¼   TEASPOON SALT

6   TABLESPOONS COLD BUTTER OR MARGARINE (¾ STICK), CUT INTO PIECES

1   TABLESPOON VEGETABLE SHORTENING

2 TO 3 TABLESPOONS ICE WATER

CHOCOLATE FILLING

6   SQUARES (6 OUNCES) SEMISWEET CHOCOLATE, COARSELY CHOPPED

½   CUP BUTTER OR MARGARINE (1 STICK)

¼   CUP SUGAR

1   TEASPOON VANILLA EXTRACT

3   LARGE EGGS

½   CUP HEAVY OR WHIPPING CREAM

SOFTLY WHIPPED CREAM (OPTIONAL)

WHITE CHOCOLATE HEARTS (PAGE 169, OPTIONAL)

1   Prepare Tart Pastry: In large bowl, combine flour and salt. With pastry blender or two knives used scissor-fashion, cut in butter and shortening until mixture resembles coarse crumbs.

2   Sprinkle in ice water, 1 tablespoon at a time, mixing lightly with a fork after each addition, until dough is just moist enough to hold together. Shape dough into disk; wrap in plastic wrap. Refrigerate 30 minutes or up to overnight. (If chilled overnight, let stand 30 minutes at room temperature before rolling.)

3   Preheat oven to 425°F. On lightly floured surface, with floured rolling pin, roll dough into 11-inch round. Gently roll dough round onto rolling pin and ease dough into 9-inch tart pan with removable bottom. Fold overhang in and press dough against side of pan so it extends ⅛ inch above rim. Refrigerate or freeze until firm, 10 to 15 minutes.

4   Line tart shell with foil; fill with pie weights or dry beans. Bake 15 minutes. Remove foil with weights; bake until golden, 5 to 10 minutes longer. If shell puffs up during baking, gently press it down with back of spoon. Cool in pan on wire rack. Turn oven control to 350°F.

5   Meanwhile, prepare Chocolate Filling: In heavy 2-quart saucepan, melt chocolate and butter over very low heat, stirring frequently, until smooth. Add sugar and vanilla, stirring until sugar has dissolved. In small bowl, with wire whisk, lightly beat eggs and cream. Whisk ⅓ cup warm chocolate

mixture into egg mixture; stir egg mixture back into chocolate mixture in saucepan until blended.

6 Pour warm chocolate filling into cooled tart shell. Bake until custard is set but center still jiggles slightly, about 20 minutes.

7 Cool in pan on wire rack, then, carefully remove side of pan. Refrigerate until chilled, about 4 hours. Decorate with white chocolate hearts, or serve with whipped cream, if desired.

EACH SERVING: ABOUT 305 CALORIES | 4G PROTEIN | 22G CARBOHYDRATE | 24G TOTAL FAT (14G SATURATED) | 1G FIBER | 103MG CHOLESTEROL | 206MG SODIUM

CHOCOLATE TRUFFLE TART WITH HAZELNUT CRUST

This luscious dessert combines a fragrant hazelnut crust with a rich and silky chocolate ganache filling.

ACTIVE TIME: 45 MINUTES · **TOTAL TIME:** 1 HOUR 30 MINUTES PLUS CHILLING AND COOLING
MAKES: 12 SERVINGS

HAZELNUT CRUST

½ CUP HAZELNUTS (FILBERTS), TOASTED (OPPOSITE)

2 TABLESPOONS SUGAR

1¼ CUPS ALL-PURPOSE FLOUR

½ TEASPOON SALT

½ CUP COLD BUTTER (1 STICK), CUT INTO PIECES (DO NOT USE MARGARINE)

4 TABLESPOONS ICE WATER

CHOCOLATE FILLING

7 SQUARES (7 OUNCES) SEMISWEET CHOCOLATE

1 SQUARE (1 OUNCE) UNSWEETENED CHOCOLATE

4 TABLESPOONS BUTTER (DO NOT USE MARGARINE)

⅓ CUP SUGAR

1 TEASPOON VANILLA EXTRACT

PINCH SALT

⅔ CUP PLUS ½ CUP HEAVY OR WHIPPING CREAM

3 LARGE EGGS

1 Prepare Hazelnut Crust: Preheat oven to 425°F. Reserve 12 whole hazelnuts for garnish. In food processor with knife blade attached, blend remaining hazelnuts with sugar until finely ground. Add flour and salt to nut mixture; pulse until blended. Scatter butter over flour; pulse just until mixture resembles coarse crumbs. With processor running, add ice water, 1 tablespoon at a time, processing until dough almost forms a ball. Shape dough into disk; wrap in plastic wrap. Refrigerate until firm, about 30 minutes.

2 On lightly floured surface, with floured rolling pin, roll dough into 14-inch round. Gently roll dough round onto rolling pin and ease into 11-inch round tart pan with removable bottom. Fold overhang in and press against side of tart pan to form a rim ⅛ inch above edge of pan. Refrigerate or freeze until firm, 10 to 20 minutes.

3 Line tart shell with foil and fill with pie weights or dry beans. Bake 20 minutes; remove foil with weights and bake until golden, 8 to 10 minutes longer. Cool tart shell in pan on wire rack. Turn oven control to 350°F.

4 Meanwhile, prepare Chocolate Filling: In heavy 3-quart saucepan, melt semisweet and unsweetened chocolates and butter over low heat, stirring frequently, until smooth. Stir in sugar, vanilla, and salt until well blended; remove from heat. In small bowl, with fork or wire whisk, lightly beat ⅔ cup cream with eggs until mixed. Gradually whisk cream mixture into chocolate mixture until blended.

5 Pour chocolate mixture into cooled tart shell. Bake until custard is just set (center will appear jiggly), 15 to 17 minutes. Cool on wire rack. Serve at room temperature or refrigerate up to 1 day. If refrigerated, let tart stand at room temperature 1 hour to soften before serving.

6 In small bowl, with mixer at medium speed, beat remaining ½ cup cream until stiff peaks form. Spoon 12 dollops of whipped cream around edge of tart; top each dollop with a reserved hazelnut.

EACH SERVING: ABOUT 500 CALORIES | 5G PROTEIN | 65G CARBOHYDRATE | 26G TOTAL FAT (16G SATURATED) | 2G FIBER | 99MG CHOLESTEROL | 428MG SODIUM

TOASTING NUTS

Toasting nuts brings out their flavor, and in the case of nuts such as hazelnuts, allows the skins to be removed.

To toast almonds, pecans, walnuts, or hazelnuts, preheat the oven to 350°F. Spread the shelled nuts in a single layer on a cookie sheet. Bake, stirring occasionally, until lightly browned and fragrant, about 10 minutes. Toast hazelnuts until the skins begin to peel away. Let the nuts cool completely before chopping.

To skin hazelnuts, wrap the still-warm nuts in a clean kitchen towel and let stand for about 10 minutes. Using the towel, rub off as much of the skin as possible (it may not all come off).

CHOCOLATE-CARAMEL WALNUT TART

If you don't have the time to refrigerate the pastry for thirty minutes, you can pop it into the freezer and it will be firm enough to roll in about half the time. Just keep an eye on it so it doesn't freeze.

ACTIVE TIME: 40 MINUTES · **TOTAL TIME:** 1 HOUR PLUS CHILLING AND COOLING
MAKES: 12 SERVINGS

TART PASTRY

1½ CUPS ALL-PURPOSE FLOUR

¼ TEASPOON SALT

½ CUP COLD BUTTER OR MARGARINE (1 STICK), CUT INTO PIECES

2 TABLESPOONS VEGETABLE SHORTENING

3 TO 5 TABLESPOONS ICE WATER

CHOCOLATE-CARAMEL FILLING

1 CUP SUGAR

¼ CUP WATER

¾ CUP HEAVY OR WHIPPING CREAM

2 BARS (4 OUNCES EACH) BITTERSWEET CHOCOLATE, COARSELY CHOPPED

2 TABLESPOONS BUTTER OR MARGARINE

2 CUPS WALNUTS (8 OUNCES), LIGHTLY TOASTED (PAGE 93) AND CHOPPED

2 TEASPOONS VANILLA EXTRACT

WHIPPED CREAM AND WALNUT HALVES

1 Prepare Tart Pastry: In large bowl, combine flour and salt. With pastry blender or two knives used scissor-fashion, cut in butter and shortening until mixture resembles coarse crumbs.

2 Sprinkle in ice water, 1 tablespoon at a time, tossing lightly with fork after each addition, until dough is just moist enough to hold together. Shape dough into disk. Wrap disk in plastic wrap. Refrigerate 30 minutes or up to overnight. (If chilled overnight, let stand at room temperature 30 minutes before rolling.)

3 On lightly floured surface, with floured rolling pin, roll dough into 14-inch round. Gently roll dough round onto rolling pin and ease into 11-inch round tart pan with removable bottom. Run small knife or rolling pin over rim of pan to remove excess dough. Refrigerate or freeze until firm, 10 to 30 minutes.

4 Preheat oven to 425°F. Line tart shell with foil; fill with pie weights or dry beans. Bake 12 minutes. Remove foil and weights; bake until golden, 10 to 12 minutes longer. If crust puffs up during baking, gently press it down with back of spoon. Cool tart shell in pan on wire rack.

5 Meanwhile, prepare Chocolate-Caramel Filling: In heavy 3-quart sauce-pan, heat sugar and water over medium-high heat until melted and amber in color, about 10 minutes, swirling pan occasionally. Remove from heat. Stir in cream until smooth caramel forms; stir in chocolate and butter until melted. Stir in chopped walnuts and vanilla.

6 Pour warm chocolate filling into cooled tart shell. Refrigerate until set, at least 3 hours. Remove side of pan to serve. Garnish with whipped cream and top with walnut halves.

EACH SERVING: ABOUT 505 CALORIES | 6G PROTEIN | 42G CARBOHYDRATE | 38G TOTAL FAT (16G SATURATED) | 3G FIBER | 48MG CHOLESTEROL | 160MG SODIUM

BROWNIE SHORTBREAD TART

Buttery shortbread meets the ultimate chocolate filling for a perfect match! Bake the tart ahead and freeze for up to a month—thaw at room temperature before serving.

ACTIVE TIME: 40 MINUTES · **TOTAL TIME:** 1 HOUR PLUS CHILLING AND COOLING
MAKES: 12 SERVINGS

SHORTBREAD CRUST (PAGE 99)

6 TABLESPOONS MARGARINE OR BUTTER (¾ STICK)

3 SQUARES (3 OUNCES) UNSWEETENED CHOCOLATE

½ CUP GRANULATED SUGAR

½ CUP PACKED LIGHT BROWN SUGAR

2 LARGE EGGS

¾ CUP ALL-PURPOSE FLOUR

⅛ TEASPOON SALT

1 TEASPOON VANILLA EXTRACT

¾ CUP PECANS, COARSELY CHOPPED

1 Prepare crust as directed. Preheat oven to 350°F.

2 In 3-quart saucepan, melt butter and chocolate over low heat, stirring frequently, until smooth. Remove from heat; stir in granulated and brown sugars. Add eggs, one at a time, stirring well after each addition. Stir in flour, salt, vanilla, and pecans until well blended. Spoon into baked crust; spread evenly.

3 Bake until top is set, 16 to 18 minutes. Cool tart in pan on wire rack 1 hour to serve warm, or cool completely to serve later.

EACH SERVING: ABOUT 370 CALORIES | 4G PROTEIN | 38G CARBOHYDRATE | 24G TOTAL FAT (12G SATURATED) | 2G FIBER | 74MG CHOLESTEROL | 185MG SODIUM

CHOCOLATE TARTLETS

If you don't have tartlet pans, not to worry. Mini muffin pans work just as well. Decorate the finished tartlets as simply or as elaborately as you like with fresh berries or sliced fruit, depending on what looks good at the market.

ACTIVE TIME: 50 MINUTES · **TOTAL TIME:** 1 HOUR PLUS CHILLING, COOLING, AND STANDING
MAKES: 36 TARTLETS

PASTRY DOUGH FOR 1-CRUST PIE (PAGE 98)

3 TABLESPOONS APRICOT JAM

2 SQUARES (2 OUNCES) SEMISWEET CHOCOLATE

3 TABLESPOONS PLUS ¼ CUP HEAVY OR WHIPPING CREAM

1 TABLESPOON BUTTER OR MARGARINE, CUT INTO PIECES

1 TEASPOON VANILLA EXTRACT

1 TEASPOON CONFECTIONERS' SUGAR

ASSORTED BERRIES, VERY THINLY SLICED KUMQUATS, OR CHOCOLATE SHAVINGS

1 Prepare dough as directed through chilling.

2 Preheat oven to 425°F. On lightly floured surface, with floured rolling pin, roll dough slightly less than ¹⁄₁₆ inch thick. With 2½-inch round cutter, cut out 36 pastry rounds (if necessary, reroll scraps). Ease into 3 dozen mini muffin-pan cups or 1¾-inch tartlet pans, pressing dough onto bottoms and against sides of pans.

3 Bake tartlet shells until golden, 9 to 12 minutes. Cool in pans on wire rack. Remove shells from pans; spoon ¼ teaspoon jam into each shell. In top of double boiler set over simmering water, melt chocolate with 3 tablespoons cream, stirring until smooth. Remove from heat; stir in butter until smooth. Stir in vanilla. Spoon mixture evenly into tartlets, covering jam. Let stand until set.

4 In small bowl, with mixer at medium speed, beat remaining ¼ cup cream and confectioners' sugar until stiff peaks form. Spoon small dollop of cream onto center of each tartlet. Garnish with berries, kumquats, or chocolate shavings.

EACH TARTLET: ABOUT 60 CALORIES | 1G PROTEIN | 5G CARBOHYDRATE | 4G TOTAL FAT (2G SATURATED) | 0G FIBER | 8MG CHOLESTEROL | 30MG SODIUM

PASTRY DOUGH FOR 1-CRUST PIE

Chilling a piecrust before baking helps it retain its shape.

TOTAL TIME: 15 MINUTES PLUS CHILLING

MAKES: ENOUGH DOUGH FOR ONE 9-INCH CRUST

1¼ CUPS ALL-PURPOSE FLOUR

¼ TEASPOON SALT

4 TABLESPOONS COLD BUTTER OR MARGARINE, CUT INTO PIECES

2 TABLESPOONS VEGETABLE SHORTENING

3 TO 5 TABLESPOONS ICE WATER

1 In large bowl, combine flour and salt. With pastry blender or two knives used scissor-fashion, cut in butter and shortening until mixture resembles coarse crumbs.

2 Sprinkle in ice water, 1 tablespoon at a time, mixing lightly with fork after each addition, until dough is just moist enough to hold together.

3 Shape dough into disk; wrap in plastic wrap. Refrigerate 30 minutes or up to overnight. (If chilled overnight, let stand 30 minutes at room temperature before rolling.)

4 On lightly floured surface, with floured rolling pin, roll dough into 12-inch round (see Tip, below). Gently roll dough round onto rolling pin and ease into pie plate, gently pressing dough against side of plate. Trim edge leaving 1-inch overhang.

5 Fold overhang under; make decorative edge (page 83). Refrigerate or freeze until firm, 10 to 15 minutes. Fill and bake as directed in recipe.

TIP To form a smooth, even round of pastry dough, roll the rolling pin outward from the center of the disk of chilled dough, then give the dough a quarter turn and again roll it outward from the center. Keep turning and rolling the dough to maintain an even overall thickness. Don't use the rolling pin to stretch the dough, just to flatten it.

EACH 1/10TH PASTRY: ABOUT 125 CALORIES | 2G PROTEIN | 13G CARBOHYDRATE | 7G TOTAL FAT (4G SATURATED) | 0.5G FIBER | 12MG CHOLESTEROL | 104MG SODIUM

SHORTBREAD CRUST

Plenty of butter, mixed with confectioners' sugar and cornstarch, gives this a melt-in-your-mouth texture.

ACTIVE TIME: 10 MINUTES · **TOTAL TIME:** 30 MINUTES PLUS CHILLING
MAKES: ENOUGH DOUGH FOR ONE 9-INCH CRUST

¾ CUP ALL-PURPOSE FLOUR

⅓ CUP CORNSTARCH

½ CUP BUTTER (1 STICK), SOFTENED
(DO NOT USE MARGARINE)

⅓ CUP CONFECTIONERS' SUGAR

1 TEASPOON VANILLA EXTRACT

1 Preheat oven to 350°F. In medium bowl, combine flour and cornstarch. In large bowl, with mixer at medium speed, beat butter and sugar until light and fluffy. Beat in vanilla. Reduce speed to low and beat in flower mixture just until evenly moistened and crumbs form.
2 Place crumbs in 9-inch tart pan with removable bottom. Place sheet of plastic wrap over crumbs and press to smooth evenly over bottom and up side of pan. Discard plastic wrap. With fork, prick bottom and side of tart shell at 1-inch intervals to prevent puffing and shrinking during baking. Refrigerate or freeze until firm, 10 to 15 minutes.
3 Bake crust until lightly browned, about 20 minutes. Transfer crust in pan to wire rack to cool.

EACH ⅛TH CRUST: ABOUT 185 CALORIES | 1G PROTEIN | 19G CARBOHYDRATE | 12G TOTAL FAT (7G SATURATED) | 0.5G FIBER | 31MG CHOLESTEROL | 120MG SODIUM

GRAHAM CRACKER CRUMB CRUST

Here's the quick classic plus two variations. Personalize your crusts by using your favorite cookies to make the crumbs.

ACTIVE TIME: 10 MINUTES · **TOTAL TIME:** 20 MINUTES
MAKES: ONE 9-INCH CRUST

1¼ CUPS GRAHAM CRACKER CRUMBS (11 RECTANGULAR GRAHAM CRACKERS)

4   TABLESPOONS BUTTER OR MARGARINE, MELTED

1   TABLESPOON SUGAR

1 Preheat oven to 375°F.

2 In 9-inch pie plate, with fork, combine crumbs, melted butter, and sugar until crumbs are evenly moistened. Press mixture firmly onto bottom and up side of pie plate, making small rim.

3 Bake 10 minutes; cool on wire rack. Fill as recipe directs.

EACH ¹/₁₀TH CRUST: ABOUT 105 CALORIES | 1G PROTEIN | 12G CARBOHYDRATE | 6G TOTAL FAT (3G SATURATED) | 0.5G FIBER | 12MG CHOLESTEROL | 137MG SODIUM

CHOCOLATE WAFER CRUMB CRUST

Prepare as directed but substitute **1¼ cups chocolate wafer crumbs** (about 24 cookies) for graham cracker crumbs.

EACH ¹/₁₀TH CRUST: ABOUT 108 CALORIES | 1G PROTEIN | 12G CARBOHYDRATE | 7G TOTAL FAT (3G SATURATED) | 0.5G FIBER | 13MG CHOLESTEROL | 130MG SODIUM

VANILLA WAFER CRUMB CRUST

Prepare as directed but substitute **1¼ cups vanilla wafer crumbs** (about 35 cookies) for graham cracker crumbs.

EACH ¹/₁₀TH CRUST: ABOUT 92 CALORIES | 1G PROTEIN | 9G CARBOHYDRATE | 6G TOTAL FAT (3G SATURATED) | 0.5G FIBER | 12MG CHOLESTEROL | 80MG SODIUM

COCONUT PASTRY CRUST

Toast the coconut in a shallow pan at 350°F for about 10 minutes, stirring frequently.

ACTIVE TIME: 10 MINUTES · **TOTAL TIME:** 30 MINUTES
MAKES: ONE 9-INCH CRUST

1 CUP ALL-PURPOSE FLOUR

½ CUP FLAKED SWEETENED COCONUT, TOASTED

6 TABLESPOONS COLD BUTTER OR MARGARINE (¾ STICK), CUT INTO PIECES

2 TABLESPOONS SUGAR

1 TABLESPOON COLD WATER

1 Preheat oven to 375°F. Grease 9-inch pie plate.

2 In food processor with knife blade attached, combine flour, coconut, butter, sugar, and cold water. Pulse until dough just holds together. Press dough evenly into bottom and up side of prepared pie plate, making a small rim.

3 Bake 20 minutes, or until golden. Cover edge loosely with foil to prevent overbrowning if necessary during last 10 minutes of baking. Cool on wire rack. Fill as recipe directs.

EACH ¹/₁₀ᴛʜ CRUST: ABOUT 135 CALORIES | 1G PROTEIN | 14G CARBOHYDRATE | 9G TOTAL FAT (5G SATURATED) | 0.5G FIBER | 19MG CHOLESTEROL | 80MG SODIUM

CRUMB CRUSTS FOR CHEESECAKES

A springform pan allows you to unmold a cheesecake with the crumb crust intact. Press the buttered crumbs evenly and firmly onto the bottom of the pan. Some recipes call for the crumbs to be pressed up the side of the pan as well (see opposite).

COOKIES & CONFECTIONS

Chocolate cookies and confections are just like compliments: They're sweet and you can never have too many. Here you'll find our most irresistible cookies, truffles, fudge, and more.

COOKIE SHEET SMARTS Good-quality cookie sheets are one of the secrets to perfect cookies. Use heavy-gauge aluminum sheets with a dull finish. Cookie sheets should be at least 2 inches smaller than your oven. For additional tips, see below:

BAKING FOR SUCCESS

- In most of our cookie recipes, either butter or margarine can be used, but for the best flavor and texture, choose butter.
- After the flour is added, mix the dough just until blended.
- Grease cookie sheets (we prefer vegetable shortening) only if directed to do so.
- Use a measuring spoon (or small ice-cream scoop) to scoop up equal portions of dough for cookies.
- For evenly baked cookies, bake one sheet of cookies at a time in the center of the oven. To bake two sheets, place them in the upper and lower thirds of the oven. Halfway through the baking, rotate the sheets from front to back and between the racks.
- Bake for the minimum suggested time, then check often for doneness.
- Unless a recipe directs otherwise, cool cookies briefly before transferring them to racks to cool completely.

STORAGE KNOW-HOW Store soft cookies and crisp cookies in separate containers with tight-fitting covers.

Florentines (page 114)

CHOCOLATE-MINT SANDWICHES

Reminiscent of a favorite Girl Scout cookie, these are popular with grown-ups and children.

ACTIVE TIME: 40 MINUTES · **TOTAL TIME:** 12 MINUTES PER BATCH PLUS COOLING
MAKES: 54 COOKIES

2 CUPS ALL-PURPOSE FLOUR	10 TABLESPOONS BUTTER OR MARGARINE (1¼ STICKS), SOFTENED
½ CUP PLUS ⅓ CUP SUGAR	¼ CUP LIGHT OR DARK CORN SYRUP
2 TEASPOONS BAKING SODA	2 LARGE EGGS
¼ TEASPOON SALT	2 BAGS (13 OUNCES EACH) CHOCOLATE-COVERED MINT PATTIES (ABOUT 54)
6 SQUARES (6 OUNCES) SEMISWEET CHOCOLATE, MELTED AND COOLED	

1 Preheat oven to 350°F. In large bowl, combine flour, ½ cup sugar, baking soda, and salt. Add melted chocolate, butter, corn syrup, and eggs. With mixer at low speed, beat until blended. Increase speed to medium; beat until well mixed, frequently scraping bowl with rubber spatula.

2 Shape dough by rounded teaspoons into balls. Roll balls in remaining ⅓ cup sugar until coated. Place balls, 2 inches apart, on ungreased large cookie sheet. Bake until set, 12 to 14 minutes. Immediately turn half of cookies over on cookie sheet. While still hot, place chocolate-covered mint patty on each inverted cookie; quickly top with remaining cookies, top side up. With wide spatula, transfer sandwich cookies to wire racks to cool 1 minute; press cookies together slightly so mint patty spreads to cookie edges as it melts. Cool cookies completely on racks.

3 Repeat with remaining dough balls, sugar, and mint patties.

EACH COOKIE: ABOUT 120 CALORIES | 1G PROTEIN | 20G CARBOHYDRATE | 4G TOTAL FAT (3G SATURATED) | 1G FIBER | 47MG CHOLESTEROL | 88MG SODIUM

CHOCOLATE MACAROON SANDWICHES

Macaroons have the most tempting texture: crisp on the outside and soft and chewy on the inside. These almond-chocolate macaroons are made even more fabulous, as they are sandwiched with a heavenly chocolate and whipped cream filling.

ACTIVE TIME: 20 MINUTES · **TOTAL TIME:** 13 MINUTES PER BATCH PLUS COOLING
MAKES: 36 COOKIES

1 CUP BLANCHED SLIVERED ALMONDS	**CHOCOLATE FILLING**
1 CUP SUGAR	¼ CUP HEAVY OR WHIPPING CREAM
2 TABLESPOONS UNSWEETENED COCOA	1½ TEASPOONS SUGAR
PINCH SALT	1 TEASPOON BUTTER OR MARGARINE
½ CUP EGG WHITES	3 OUNCES BITTERSWEET CHOCOLATE OR 3 SQUARES (3 OUNCES) SEMISWEET CHOCOLATE, CHOPPED
2 SQUARES (2 OUNCES) UNSWEETENED CHOCOLATE, MELTED AND COOLED	
½ TEASPOON VANILLA EXTRACT	¼ TEASPOON VANILLA EXTRACT

1 Preheat oven to 350°F. Line two large cookie sheets with parchment paper.
2 In food processor with knife blade attached, combine almonds, sugar, cocoa, and salt; process until almonds are ground to a powder. Add egg whites, melted chocolate, and vanilla; process until a paste is formed.
3 Transfer batter to large pastry bag fitted with ¾-inch round tip. Pipe batter into 1-inch mounds, 2 inches apart, on prepared cookie sheets. Bake until almost firm, 13 to 14 minutes. Cool macaroons 1 minute on cookie sheets on wire racks. With wide spatula, carefully transfer macaroons to racks to cool completely.
4 Prepare Chocolate Filling: In 1-quart saucepan, combine cream, sugar, and butter; heat to boiling over medium-high heat. Remove from heat. Add chocolate to cream mixture; stir until melted and smooth. Stir in vanilla. Pour into small shallow bowl; refrigerate until firm and spreadable, at least 1 hour.
5 Turn half of macaroons so flat bottoms face up. With small metal spatula, spread scant 2 teaspoons chocolate filling on each macaroon. Place remaining macaroons on top to make sandwiches.

EACH COOKIE: ABOUT 290 CALORIES | 3G PROTEIN | 31G CARBOHYDRATE | 18G TOTAL FAT (11G SATURATED) | 1G FIBER | 66MG CHOLESTEROL | 95MG SODIUM

WHOOPIE PIES

You may remember these yummy treats from your childhood: soft, cake-like cookies that are sandwiched with fluffy marshallow crème.

ACTIVE TIME: 30 MINUTES · **TOTAL TIME:** 40 MINUTES PLUS COOLING
MAKES: 12 WHOOPIE PIES

---

2   CUPS ALL-PURPOSE FLOUR

1   CUP SUGAR

½   CUP UNSWEETENED COCOA

1   TEASPOON BAKING SODA

¼   TEASPOON SALT

¾   CUP MILK

6   TABLESPOONS BUTTER OR MARGARINE (¾ STICK), MELTED

1   LARGE EGG

1   TEASPOON VANILLA EXTRACT

MARSHMALLOW CRÈME FILLING (BELOW)

1   Preheat oven to 350°F. Grease two large cookie sheets.

2   In large bowl, with wooden spoon, combine flour, sugar, cocoa, baking soda, and salt. Add milk, butter, egg, and vanilla; stir until smooth.

3   Drop 12 heaping tablespoons batter, 2 inches apart, on each prepared cookie sheet.

4   Bake until puffy and toothpick inserted in center comes out clean, 12 to 14 minutes, rotating cookie sheets between upper and lower racks halfway through baking time. With wide spatula, transfer cookies to wire racks to cool completely.

5   When cool, prepare Marshmallow Crème Filling. Spread 1 rounded tablespoon filling over flat side of 12 cookies. Top with remaining cookies, flat side down, to make 12 sandwiches.

MARSHMALLOW CRÈME FILLING

In large bowl, with mixer at medium speed, beat **6 tablespoons butter or margarine**, slightly softened, until creamy. With mixer at low speed, gradually beat in **1 cup confectioners' sugar** until blended. Beat in **1 jar (7 to 7½-ounces) marshmallow crème** (about 1½ cups) and **1 teaspoon vanilla extract** until well combined.

EACH WHOOPIE PIE: ABOUT 360 CALORIES | 4G PROTEIN | 60G CARBOHYDRATE | 13G TOTAL FAT (8G SATURATED) | 1.5G FIBER | 51MG CHOLESTEROL | 289MG SODIUM

DOUBLE CHOCOLATE–CHERRY DROPS

The subtle tartness of the cherries provides a delicious contrast to the double dose of rich chocolate from semisweet chunks and cocoa.

ACTIVE TIME: 25 MINUTES · **TOTAL TIME:** 10 MINUTES PER BATCH PLUS COOLING
MAKES: 60 COOKIES

1¾ CUPS ALL-PURPOSE FLOUR

¾ CUP UNSWEETENED COCOA

¼ TEASPOON SALT

1 CUP BUTTER OR MARGARINE
(2 STICKS), SOFTENED

1 CUP SUGAR

¼ CUP LIGHT CORN SYRUP

1 LARGE EGG

2 TEASPOONS VANILLA EXTRACT

1 PACKAGE (8 OUNCES) SEMISWEET-
CHOCOLATE SQUARES OR 8 OUNCES
WHITE CHOCOLATE, CUT INTO ½-
INCH PIECES

1 CUP DRIED TART CHERRIES

1 Preheat oven to 350°F. In medium bowl, combine flour, cocoa, and salt.

2 In large bowl, with mixer at medium speed, beat butter and sugar until creamy, occasionally scraping bowl with rubber spatula. Beat in corn syrup, egg, and vanilla until well mixed. Reduce speed to low. Gradually add flour mixture; beat just until blended, occasionally scraping bowl. With wooden spoon, stir in chocolate and cherries.

3 Drop cookies by rounded teaspoons, 2 inches apart, onto ungreased cookie sheet. Bake until tops are just firm, 10 to 11 minutes. With wide spatula, transfer cookies to wire racks to cool completely.

4 Repeat with remaining dough.

EACH COOKIE: ABOUT 85 CALORIES | 1G PROTEIN | 11G CARBOHYDRATE | 5G TOTAL FAT
(3G SATURATED) | 1G FIBER | 12MG CHOLESTEROL | 50MG SODIUM

DOUBLE-CHOCOLATE CHUNK COOKIES

We love these cookies for the bigger-than-usual chunks of chocolate they contain. You can use packaged chocolate chunks as we did here or purchase high-quality chocolate and cut it up.

ACTIVE TIME: 30 MINUTES · **TOTAL TIME:** 14 MINUTES PER BATCH
MAKES: 18 COOKIES

¼ CUP ALL-PURPOSE FLOUR

¼ CUP UNSWEETENED COCOA

½ TEASPOON BAKING POWDER

¼ TEASPOON SALT

8 SQUARES (8 OUNCES) SEMISWEET CHOCOLATE, CHOPPED

6 TABLESPOONS BUTTER OR MARGARINE, CUT INTO PIECES

1 CUP SUGAR

2 TEASPOONS VANILLA EXTRACT

2 LARGE EGGS

1 PACKAGE (6 OUNCES) SEMISWEET CHOCOLATE CHUNKS

½ CUP PECANS, CHOPPED

½ CUP WALNUTS, CHOPPED

1 Preheat oven to 350°F. In small bowl, combine flour, cocoa, baking powder, and salt.

2 In 3-quart saucepan, melt chopped chocolate and butter over low heat, stirring frequently, until smooth. Pour into large bowl; cool to lukewarm. Stir in sugar and vanilla until blended. Stir in eggs, one at a time, until well blended. Add flour mixture; stir until combined (batter will be thin). Stir in chocolate chunks, pecans, and walnuts.

3 Drop batter by heaping tablespoons, 1½ inches apart, on ungreased large cookie sheet. Bake until set, about 14 minutes. Cool on cookie sheet on wire rack 2 minutes. With wide spatula, carefully transfer cookies to racks to cool completely.

4 Repeat with remaining dough.

EACH COOKIE: ABOUT 360 CALORIES | 5G PROTEIN | 37G CARBOHYDRATE | 24G TOTAL FAT (3G SATURATED) | 3G FIBER | 12MG CHOLESTEROL | 255MG SODIUM

APRICOT FUDGIES

Nestlé introduced the first American white chocolate bar in 1987. It quickly became available in supermarkets across the country, and we were infatuated with it—in sauces, cheesecakes, and chunky cookies. Here white chocolate chunks and chopped dried apricots come together in a delectable fudge cookie.

ACTIVE TIME: 30 MINUTES · **TOTAL TIME:** 13 MINUTES PER BATCH PLUS COOLING
MAKES: 36 COOKIES

¼ CUP ALL-PURPOSE FLOUR

¼ CUP UNSWEETENED COCOA

½ TEASPOON BAKING POWDER

¼ TEASPOON SALT

8 SQUARES (8 OUNCES) SEMISWEET CHOCOLATE, COARSELY CHOPPED

6 TABLESPOONS BUTTER OR MARGARINE (¾ STICK), CUT INTO PIECES

¾ CUP SUGAR

2 TEASPOONS VANILLA EXTRACT

2 LARGE EGGS

6 OUNCES WHITE CHOCOLATE, SWISS CONFECTIONERY BAR, OR WHITE BAKING BAR, COARSELY CHOPPED

1 CUP DRIED APRICOT HALVES (ABOUT 8 OUNCES), COARSELY CHOPPED

1 Preheat oven to 350°F. In small bowl, combine flour, cocoa, baking powder, and salt.

2 In 3-quart saucepan, melt semisweet chocolate and butter over low heat, stirring frequently, until smooth. Remove from heat; with wire whisk, stir in sugar and vanilla until blended. Whisk in eggs, one at a time, until mixture is smooth. With wooden spoon, stir flour mixture into chocolate mixture until combined. Add white chocolate and apricots; stir just until evenly mixed (dough will be loose and sticky).

3 Drop dough by rounded tablespoons, 1½ inches apart, onto ungreased large cookie sheet. Bake until tops of cookies are set, 13 to 15 minutes. Cool 30 seconds on cookie sheet. With wide spatula, transfer cookies to wire rack to cool completely.

4 Repeat with remaining dough.

EACH COOKIE: ABOUT 500 CALORIES | 5G PROTEIN | 65G CARBOHYDRATE | 26G TOTAL FAT (16G SATURATED) | 2G FIBER | 99MG CHOLESTEROL | 428MG SODIUM

DOUBLE-CHOCOLATE BISCOTTI

These classic crunchy Italian cookies are delectable with a mug of freshly brewed coffee or a glass of ice-cold milk.

ACTIVE TIME: 30 MINUTES · **TOTAL TIME:** 1 HOUR 20 MINUTES PLUS COOLING
MAKES: 36 BISCOTTI

2½ CUPS ALL-PURPOSE FLOUR

¾ CUP UNSWEETENED COCOA

1 TABLESPOON BAKING POWDER

½ TEASPOON SALT

½ CUP BUTTER OR MARGARINE (1 STICK), SOFTENED

1⅓ CUPS SUGAR

3 LARGE EGGS

2 SQUARES (2 OUNCES) SEMISWEET CHOCOLATE, MELTED

1 TEASPOON INSTANT ESPRESSO-COFFEE POWDER

1 TEASPOON HOT WATER

¾ CUP SEMISWEET CHOCOLATE MINI CHIPS

1 Preheat oven to 350°F. Grease and flour large cookie sheet. In large bowl combine flour, cocoa, baking powder, and salt.

2 In another large bowl, with mixer at medium speed, beat butter and sugar until creamy. Reduce speed to low. Add eggs, one at a time, beating well after each addition. Add melted chocolate; beat until well combined.

3 In cup, dissolve espresso powder in hot water; beat into chocolate mixture. Add flour mixture; beat just until blended. With hands, knead in chocolate chips until combined.

4 On floured surface, with floured hands, divide dough in half. Shape each piece of dough into 12" by 3" log. With pastry brush, brush off excess flour. Place logs, 3 inches apart, on cookie sheet. Bake 30 minutes. Cool logs on cookie sheet on wire rack 10 minutes.

5 Transfer 1 log to cutting board. With serrated knife, cut log crosswise on diagonal into ¾-inch-thick slices. Repeat with remaining log. Place slices, cut side down, on same cookie sheet. Bake 20 to 25 minutes to dry biscotti. With wide spatula, transfer biscotti to wire racks to cool completely. (Biscotti will harden as they cool.)

EACH COOKIE: ABOUT 115 CALORIES | 2G PROTEIN | 19G CARBOHYDRATE | 4G TOTAL FAT (2G SATURATED) | 1G FIBER | 25MG CHOLESTEROL | 97MG SODIUM

CHOCOLATE PRETZELS

Making these pretzel-shaped treats is a perfect project for kids and parents.

ACTIVE TIME: 1 HOUR · **TOTAL TIME:** 15 MINUTES PER BATCH PLUS COOLING
MAKES: 36 PRETZELS

2	CUPS ALL-PURPOSE FLOUR	¾	CUP SUGAR
⅓	CUP UNSWEETENED COCOA	1	LARGE EGG
2	TEASPOONS BAKING POWDER	1	TEASPOON VANILLA EXTRACT
½	TEASPOON SALT		ASSORTED SPRINKLES
¾	CUP BUTTER OR MARGARINE (1½ STICKS), SOFTENED		

1 Preheat oven to 350°F. In medium bowl, combine flour, cocoa, baking powder, and salt.

2 In large bowl, with mixer at medium speed, beat butter and sugar until creamy. Beat in egg and vanilla until well blended. At low speed, beat in flour mixture just until blended, occasionally scraping bowl with rubber spatula.

3 Divide dough in half. Wrap one piece of dough in plastic. Place sprinkles in pie plate.

4 Working with unwrapped portion of dough, on unfloured work surface, with hands shape tablespoons of dough into 9-inch-long ropes. Shape ropes into loop-shaped pretzels; press ends lightly to seal. Gently press pretzels, top side down, into sprinkles. Place pretzels, decorated side up, ½ inch apart, on ungreased large cookie sheet.

5 Bake pretzels until bottoms are lightly browned, about 15 minutes. With wide spatula, transfer pretzels to wire racks to cool completely.

6 Repeat with remaining piece of dough.

EACH PRETZEL: ABOUT 80 CALORIES | 1G PROTEIN | 10G CARBOHYDRATE | 4G TOTAL FAT (3G SATURATED) | 0.5G FIBER | 16MG CHOLESTEROL | 93MG SODIUM

FLORENTINES

Made with very little flour—but lots of almonds and candied orange peel—these elegant cookies are perfect for a reception or a special gift. Handle the cookies carefully when icing them, as they are quite fragile. For an even more lavish treat, sandwich two cookies together with a layer of chocolate in between. (For photo, see page 102.)

ACTIVE TIME: 40 MINUTES · **TOTAL TIME:** 10 MINUTES PER BATCH PLUS COOLING
MAKES: 48 COOKIES

6   TABLESPOONS BUTTER (¾ STICK), CUT INTO PIECES (DO NOT USE MARGARINE)

¼   CUP HEAVY OR WHIPPING CREAM

1   TABLESPOON LIGHT CORN SYRUP

½   CUP SUGAR

2   TABLESPOONS ALL-PURPOSE FLOUR

1   CUP SLIVERED ALMONDS (4 OUNCES), FINELY CHOPPED

½   CUP CANDIED ORANGE PEEL, FINELY CHOPPED

8   SQUARES (8 OUNCES) SEMISWEET CHOCOLATE, MELTED

1   Preheat oven to 350°F. Line large cookie sheet with cooking parchment.

2   In 1-quart saucepan, combine butter, cream, corn syrup, sugar, and flour. Heat to boiling over medium heat, stirring frequently. Remove from heat; stir in almonds and candied orange peel.

3   Drop batter by rounded teaspoons, 3 inches apart, on prepared cookie sheet. Do not place more than 6 cookies on sheet. Bake just until set, about 10 minutes. Cool on cookie sheet on wire rack 1 minute. With wide spatula, transfer to racks to cool. If cookies become too hard to remove; return sheet to oven briefly to soften. Repeat with remaining batter.

4   With small metal spatula or butter knife, spread flat side of cookie with melted chocolate. Return to racks, chocolate side up; let stand until chocolate sets.

EACH COOKIE: ABOUT 70 CALORIES | 1G PROTEIN | 8G CARBOHYDRATE | 5G TOTAL FAT (2G SATURATED) | 0G FIBER | 6MG CHOLESTEROL | 15MG SODIUM

CHOCOLATE PANFORTE

This rich, dense confection is a specialty of Siena, Italy. It's delicious with an espresso or as an accompaniment to cheese.

ACTIVE TIME: 30 MINUTES · **TOTAL TIME:** 50 MINUTES PLUS COOLING AND STANDING
MAKES: 24 SERVINGS

¼ CUP ALL-PURPOSE FLOUR

¼ CUP UNSWEETENED COCOA

3 OUNCES BITTERSWEET CHOCOLATE, GRATED, OR ½ CUP SEMISWEET CHOCOLATE CHIPS

½ TEASPOON GROUND CINNAMON

⅛ TEASPOON GROUND CLOVES

⅛ TEASPOON GROUND GINGER

⅛ TEASPOON GROUND NUTMEG

¾ CUP CHOPPED CANDIED ORANGE PEEL

1 TABLESPOON GRATED FRESH ORANGE PEEL

1 CUP BLANCHED ALMONDS (4 OUNCES), TOASTED AND COARSELY CHOPPED

1 CUP HAZELNUTS (4 OUNCES), TOASTED, SKINNED (PAGE 93), AND COARSELY CHOPPED

¾ CUP PACKED LIGHT BROWN SUGAR

⅓ CUP HONEY

2 TABLESPOONS UNSALTED BUTTER OR MARGARINE

1 TABLESPOON WATER

CONFECTIONERS' SUGAR

1 Preheat oven to 325°F. Line 9-inch pie pan or 8-inch round cake pan with foil, extending foil over rim of pan. Lightly oil foil.

2 In large bowl, combine flour, cocoa, chocolate, cinnamon, cloves, ginger, nutmeg, candied and fresh orange peel, almonds, and hazelnuts.

3 In heavy 2-quart saucepan, combine brown sugar, honey, butter, and water; stir until blended. Heat to rolling boil over medium heat. Boil, stirring constantly, 1 minute. Remove from heat; immediately pour hot sugar mixture over chocolate-nut mixture, stirring to coat nuts. Pour into prepared pan; spread to form smooth, even layer.

4 Bake until panforte starts to bubble around edge, about 20 minutes. Place panforte in pan on wire rack. Cool completely.

5 Remove panforte from pan by lifting edges of foil; peel away foil. Invert onto rack. Wrap in foil. Store in airtight container at room temperature up to 1 week or refrigerate up to 3 weeks. (Age for at least 1 day before serving.)

6 To serve, unwrap panforte. Stencil small stars on top (page 170). Slice panforte into thin wedges.

EACH SERVING: ABOUT 155 CALORIES | 3G PROTEIN | 20G CARBOHYDRATE | 8G TOTAL FAT (2G SATURATED) | 2G FIBER | 3MG CHOLESTEROL | 5MG SODIUM

CHOCOLATE TRUFFLES

To add extra flavor to these easy-to-make bittersweet confections, stir two tablespoons of a favorite liqueur, such as Grand Marnier, or brandy into the melted chocolate mixture.

TOTAL TIME: 25 MINUTES PLUS CHILLING

MAKES: 32 TRUFFLES

8   OUNCES BITTERSWEET CHOCOLATE OR 6 SQUARES (6 OUNCES) SEMISWEET CHOCOLATE PLUS 2 SQUARES (2 OUNCES) UNSWEETENED CHOCOLATE

½   CUP HEAVY OR WHIPPING CREAM

3   TABLESPOONS UNSALTED BUTTER, CUT INTO PIECES AND SOFTENED (DO NOT USE MARGARINE)

⅓   CUP HAZELNUTS (FILBERTS), TOASTED AND SKINNED (PAGE 93), FINELY CHOPPED

3   TABLESPOONS UNSWEETENED COCOA

1 Line 9" by 5" metal loaf pan with plastic wrap. In food processor with knife blade attached, process chocolate until finely ground.

2 In 1-quart saucepan, heat cream to boiling over medium-high heat. Add cream to chocolate in food processor; process until smooth. Add butter; process to blend well.

3 Pour chocolate mixture into prepared pan; spread evenly. Refrigerate until cool and firm enough to handle, about 3 hours.

4 Place hazelnuts in small bowl, place cocoa in another small bowl. Lift chocolate mixture from pan by holding edges of plastic wrap; invert chocolate block onto cutting board. Discard plastic. Cut chocolate block into 32 pieces. (To cut chocolate mixture easily, dip knife in hot water and wipe dry.) With cool hands, quickly roll each piece into a ball. One at a time, roll half of balls in hazelnuts and roll remaining balls in cocoa. Place in single layer in waxed paper–lined airtight container. Refrigerate up to 1 week or freeze up to 1 month. Remove from freezer 5 minutes before serving.

EACH TRUFFLE: ABOUT 65 CALORIES | 1G PROTEIN | 5G CARBOHYDRATE | 6G TOTAL FAT (3G SATURATED) | 1G FIBER | 8MG CHOLESTEROL | 2MG SODIUM

MOCHA TRUFFLES

Make these truffles up to two weeks ahead—they're perfect for holiday gift-giving.

TOTAL TIME: 30 MINUTES PLUS CHILLING

MAKES: 48 TRUFFLES

12 SQUARES (12 OUNCES) SEMISWEET CHOCOLATE, COARSELY CHOPPED

¾ CUP SWEETENED CONDENSED MILK

1 TABLESPOON INSTANT-COFFEE POWDER OR GRANULES

2 TABLESPOONS COFFEE-FLAVORED LIQUEUR

⅛ TEASPOON SALT

½ CUP UNSWEETENED COCOA

1 In heavy 2-quart saucepan, melt chocolate over low heat, stirring frequently, until smooth. Stir in sweetened condensed milk, coffee powder, liqueur, and salt until well mixed. Refrigerate mixture until easy to shape, about 30 minutes.

2 Place cocoa in small bowl. Dust hands with cocoa, then shape 1 rounded teaspoon chocolate mixture into a ball. Dip ball in cocoa to coat. Repeat with remaining chocolate mixture. Place truffles in single layer in waxed paper–lined airtight container. Refrigerate up to 2 weeks or freeze up to 1 month. Remove from freezer 5 minutes before serving.

EACH TRUFFLE: ABOUT 55 CALORIES | 1G PROTEIN | 7G CARBOHYDRATE | 3G TOTAL FAT (2G SATURATED) | 1G FIBER | 2MG CHOLESTEROL | 10MG SODIUM

AMARETTO TRUFFLES

This recipe is so easy to prepare, you'll be able to make many batches to give to all your friends and family for the holidays. Place each truffle in a fluted foil or paper cup.

TOTAL TIME: 25 MINUTES PLUS CHILLING
MAKES: 64 TRUFFLES

10 SQUARES (10 OUNCES) SEMISWEET CHOCOLATE	5 TABLESPOONS UNSALTED BUTTER, CUT INTO PIECES AND SOFTENED (DO NOT USE MARGARINE)
2 SQUARES (2 OUNCES) UNSWEETENED CHOCOLATE	¼ CUP ALMOND-FLAVORED LIQUEUR
¾ CUP HEAVY OR WHIPPING CREAM	⅓ CUP BLANCHED ALMONDS, TOASTED (PAGE 93) AND FINELY CHOPPED
	¼ CUP UNSWEETENED COCOA

1 Grease 8-inch square baking pan; line with plastic wrap. In food processor with knife blade attached, process semisweet and unsweetened chocolates until very finely ground.

2 In 1-quart saucepan, heat cream to boiling over medium-high heat. With food processor running, add hot cream, butter, and liqueur to chocolate; blend until smooth.

3 Pour chocolate mixture into pan; spread evenly. Refrigerate chocolate mixture until cool and firm enough to handle, at least 3 hours, or freeze 1 hour.

4 Place chopped almonds in small bowl; place cocoa in another small bowl. Invert chocolate block onto cutting board; discard plastic wrap. Cut chocolate block into 8 strips, then cut each strip crosswise into 8 squares. (To cut chocolate block neatly, dip knife in hot water and wipe dry.)

5 Roll half of chocolate squares, one at a time, in chopped almonds and remaining squares in cocoa. Place truffles in single layer in waxed paper–lined airtight container. Refrigerate up to 2 weeks or freeze up to 1 month. Remove from freezer 5 minutes before serving.

EACH TRUFFLE: ABOUT 55 CALORIES | 1G PROTEIN | 4G CARBOHYDRATE | 4G TOTAL FAT (2G SATURATED) | 1G FIBER | 6MG CHOLESTEROL | 1MG SODIUM

PEANUT BUTTER CUPS

Just enough for two bites—a luscious homemade version of everyone's favorite candy.

TOTAL TIME: 40 MINUTES PLUS CHILLING

MAKES: 60 CANDIES

---

9   OUNCES WHITE CHOCOLATE, SWISS CONFECTIONERY BARS, OR WHITE BAKING BARS, CHOPPED

1½ CUPS CREAMY PEANUT BUTTER

8   SQUARES (8 OUNCES) SEMISWEET CHOCOLATE, CHOPPED

⅓   CUP LIGHTLY SALTED PEANUTS, CHOPPED

1   Arrange 60 miniature (1" by ¼") baking cups in jelly-roll pan.

2   In heavy 2-quart saucepan, heat white chocolate and ¾ cup peanut butter over low heat, stirring occasionally, until melted and smooth. Divide peanut butter mixture evenly among baking cups. Refrigerate 10 minutes.

3   Meanwhile, in heavy 2-quart saucepan, heat semisweet chocolate and remaining ¾ cup peanut butter over low heat, stirring occasionally, until melted and smooth.

4   Spoon warm chocolate–peanut butter mixture on top of chilled mixture in baking cups; sprinkle with peanuts. Refrigerate overnight. Store candies in airtight container in single layer. Refrigerate for up to 1 week or freeze up to 1 month.

EACH CANDY: ABOUT 85 CALORIES │ 2G PROTEIN │ 7G CARBOHYDRATE │ 6G TOTAL FAT (2G SATURATED) │ 1G FIBER │ 1MG CHOLESTEROL │ 40MG SODIUM

PEANUT-CHOCOLATE BALLS

Finely chopped peanuts add a crunchy coating to these rich candies.

ACTIVE TIME: 45 MINUTES · **TOTAL TIME:** 50 MINUTES PLUS CHILLING
MAKES: 72 CANDIES

---

1 CUP CREAMY PEANUT BUTTER

1 CUP CONFECTIONERS' SUGAR

1 TABLESPOON HONEY

6 SQUARES (6 OUNCES) SEMISWEET CHOCOLATE, COARSELY CHOPPED

1 TABLESPOON VEGETABLE SHORTENING

2 CUPS DRY-ROASTED PEANUTS, FINELY CHOPPED

1 Line jelly-roll pan with waxed paper. In medium bowl stir peanut butter, confectioners' sugar, and honey until well blended, kneading with hands if necessary.

2 Shape peanut butter mixture into ¾-inch balls; place in jelly-roll pan. Cover and refrigerate until firm, about 2 hours.

3 When peanut butter balls are firm, in 1-quart saucepan, melt chocolate and shortening over low heat, stirring frequently, until smooth. Remove from heat; cool slightly.

4 Place chopped peanuts in small bowl. With fork, carefully dip peanut butter balls into chocolate mixture. Then, using same fork, roll balls in peanuts to coat. Return coated balls to jelly-roll pan. Loosely cover pan; refrigerate until coating sets, about 1 hour. Layer between waxed paper in airtight container. Refrigerate up to 2 weeks.

EACH CANDY: ABOUT 65 CALORIES | 2G PROTEIN | 5G CARBOHYDRATE | 5G TOTAL FAT (1G SATURATED) | 1G FIBER | 0MG CHOLESTEROL | 50MG SODIUM

CRACKLY CHOCOLATE ALMONDS

Toasting almonds accomplishes two things: It crisps them up and brings out their flavor.

ACTIVE TIME: 1 HOUR 10 MINUTES · **TOTAL TIME:** 1 HOUR 25 MINUTES PLUS COOLING
MAKES: 8 CUPS

4 CUPS WHOLE BLANCHED ALMONDS (1 POUND)	1 TEASPOON VANILLA EXTRACT
1¼ CUPS SUGAR	1 POUND BITTERSWEET OR SEMISWEET CHOCOLATE, CHOPPED
¼ CUP WATER	⅓ CUP UNSWEETENED COCOA

1 Preheat oven to 350°F. Spread almonds in two jelly-roll pans or on two cookie sheets. Bake, stirring occasionally, until toasted, 15 minutes. Cool.

2 Line same pans with parchment or foil. In heavy 4-quart saucepan, combine almonds, sugar, water, and vanilla. Cook, stirring constantly, over medium-high heat until sugar is thick and cloudy and crystallizes on side of pan and almonds are coated and separate, 5 to 6 minutes. With slotted spoon, transfer almonds to jelly-roll pans, leaving excess sugar in saucepan. Spread almonds out; refrigerate until cold, about 45 minutes.

3 Meanwhile, in large microwave-safe bowl, melt half of chopped chocolate in microwave oven on High for 1½ to 2 minutes; stir until smooth. Cool slightly.

4 With hands, transfer almonds from one pan to chocolate in bowl; discard any excess sugar in pan. With wooden spoon, stir until almonds are completely coated with chocolate. Line same jelly-roll pan with parchment paper; spoon almonds into pan. With fork, spread out almonds and separate as much as possible. Repeat with remaining chocolate and almonds. Refrigerate until chocolate is set, about 1 hour.

5 Sift cocoa into large bowl. Break almonds apart if necessary. Add almonds, in batches, to cocoa, tossing to coat well. (If you want variations in color, toss about three-fourths of the almonds in cocoa and leave the remaining nuts uncoated.) Place cocoa-coated almonds in sieve and gently shake to remove excess cocoa. Place almonds in airtight container. Refrigerate up to 1 month.

EACH ¼ CUP: ABOUT 175 CALORIES | 4G PROTEIN | 16G CARBOHYDRATE | 12G TOTAL FAT (3G SATURATED) | 3G FIBER | 0MG CHOLESTEROL | 2MG SODIUM

CREAMY FUDGE

A silky-smooth candy treat you can make up to one month ahead and freeze to enjoy later.

ACTIVE TIME: 10 MINUTES · **TOTAL TIME:** 15 MINUTES PLUS CHILLING
MAKES: 64 PIECES

---

16 SQUARES (16 OUNCES) SEMISWEET CHOCOLATE, CHOPPED

1 SQUARE (1 OUNCE) UNSWEETENED CHOCOLATE, CHOPPED

1 CAN (14 OUNCES) SWEETENED CONDENSED MILK

1½ TEASPOONS VANILLA EXTRACT

⅛ TEASPOON SALT

1 Line 8-inch square baking pan with foil, extending foil above rim of opposite sides.

2 In 2-quart saucepan, combine semisweet and unsweetened chocolates and condensed milk. Cook, stirring constantly, over medium-low heat until chocolates have melted and mixture is smooth, about 5 minutes.

3 Remove saucepan from heat; stir in vanilla and salt. Pour chocolate mixture into prepared pan; spread evenly. Refrigerate until firm, at least 4 hours or up to overnight.

4 Remove fudge from pan by lifting edges of foil. Invert fudge onto cutting board; discard foil. Cut into 8 strips, then cut each strip crosswise into 8 pieces. Place pieces between waxed paper in airtight container. Store at room temperature up to 1 week, or refrigerate up to 1 month.

EACH PIECE: ABOUT 55 CALORIES | 1G PROTEIN | 8G CARBOHYDRATE | 3G TOTAL FAT (2G SATURATED) | 1G FIBER | 2MG CHOLESTEROL | 15MG SODIUM

CHOCOLATE-WALNUT FUDGE

Prepare fudge as directed but stir in **1 cup walnuts (4 ounces)**, coarsely chopped, along with vanilla and salt.

EACH PIECE: ABOUT 65 CALORIES | 1G PROTEIN | 8G CARBOHYDRATE | 4G TOTAL FAT (2G SATURATED) | 1G FIBER | 2MG CHOLESTEROL | 13MG SODIUM

CHUNKY BLACK AND WHITE CHOCOLATE BARK

Studded with dried cranberries and pistachio nuts, our version of chocolate bark is the perfect holiday treat. Pack it into small boxes or cellophane bags and tie them up with red and green ribbons.

TOTAL TIME: 20 MINUTES PLUS CHILLING

MAKES: 1¾ POUNDS

---

1   CUP SHELLED PISTACHIOS (ABOUT 8 OUNCES UNSHELLED)

12 SQUARES (12 OUNCES) SEMISWEET CHOCOLATE, CHOPPED

8   OUNCES WHITE CHOCOLATE, SWISS CONFECTIONERY BARS, OR WHITE BAKING BARS, CHOPPED

¾   CUP DRIED CRANBERRIES

1   Preheat oven to 350°F. Place pistachios in medium baking pan; toast in oven, stirring occasionally, until lightly browned, 10 to 15 minutes. Cool in pan on wire rack.

2   Meanwhile in 2-quart saucepan, melt semisweet chocolate over low heat, stirring frequently, until smooth. In 1-quart saucepan, melt white chocolate over low heat, stirring frequently, until smooth. Remove pans from heat.

3   In small bowl, combine pistachios and cranberries. Stir half of nut mixture into semisweet chocolate. On large cookie sheet, with small metal spatula, spread semisweet-chocolate mixture to about ¼-inch thickness. Drop white chocolate by tablespoons on top of semisweet chocolate mixture. With tip of knife, swirl chocolates together for marbled effect. Sprinkle with remaining nut mixture. Refrigerate until firm, about 1 hour. Break bark into pieces. Layer between waxed paper in airtight container. Refrigerate up to 1 month.

EACH OUNCE: ABOUT 140 CALORIES | 2G PROTEIN | 16G CARBOHYDRATE | 9G TOTAL FAT (4G SATURATED) | 2G FIBER | 1MG CHOLESTEROL | 10MG SODIUM

CHOCOLATE-DIPPED DRIED FRUIT

This recipe can be doubled to make enough to serve a crowd. After several tries, we found that it is easiest if the larger pieces of fruit are dipped first. Use the smaller pieces to scrape up the melted chocolate remaining in the pan. We used dried apricots, apples, pears, and pineapple, but you can use other fruits, such as peaches and mango.

ACTIVE TIME: 10 MINUTES · **TOTAL TIME:** 15 MINUTES PLUS COOLING
MAKES: 33 PIECES DIPPED FRUIT

---

4   SQUARES (4 OUNCES) SEMISWEET CHOCOLATE, CHOPPED

1   TEASPOON VEGETABLE SHORTENING

1   POUND MIXED DRIED FRUIT, SUCH AS APRICOTS, APPLES, PEARS, AND PINEAPPLE

3   OUNCES CRYSTALLIZED GINGER (OPTIONAL)

1   Place sheet of waxed paper under large wire rack. In top of double boiler or in small metal bowl set over 2-quart saucepan (double-boiler top or bowl should be 2 inches above water), melt chocolate and shortening, stirring frequently, until smooth.

2   With fingers, dip one piece of fruit at a time halfway into chocolate. Shake off excess chocolate or gently scrape fruit across rim of double boiler, being careful not to remove too much chocolate. Place dipped fruit on wire rack; allow chocolate to set, at least 1 hour.

3   Layer fruit between sheets of waxed paper in airtight container. Store at room temperature up to 1 week.

EACH SERVING: ABOUT 55 CALORIES | 1G PROTEIN | 12G CARBOHYDRATE | 1G TOTAL FAT (1G SATURATED) | 1G FIBER | 0MG CHOLESTEROL | 2MG SODIUM

MORE CHOCOLATY DESSERTS

This may well become your favorite chapter. It is filled with silky puddings, light-as-a-feather soufflés, and the most luscious ice-cream desserts ever.

CUSTARDS AND PUDDINGS Custards need moderate cooking temperature, so they are always baked in a hot water bath, a roasting pan filled with enough hot water to come halfway up the side of the custard.

SOUFFLÉ SAVVY The secret to a high-rising soufflé is perfectly beaten egg whites. The egg whites beat to their highest volume at room temperature, but eggs separate most easily when cold. The key is to separate the cold eggs, then let them stand at room temperature for about 30 minutes. Beat egg whites just until stiff—not dry. Overbeaten whites look cottony and clumpy. For additional tips, see page 53.

MERINGUE MAGIC For best results, don't try to make meringue on a humid day. Before you begin, make sure the bowl and beaters do not have any fat on them. Beat the egg whites until soft peaks form, then gradually add the sugar, beating until stiff peaks form. When you think you are done, rub a bit of meringue between your fingers to be sure the sugar has dissolved.

Brownie Baked Alaska (page 156)

CHOCOLATE SOUFFLÉS

Soufflés are always impressive. They are irresistible as individual soufflés and spectacular when baked as one large dessert.

ACTIVE TIME: 20 MINUTES · TOTAL TIME: 45 MINUTES
MAKES: 8 INDIVIDUAL SOUFFLÉS

1¼ CUPS PLUS 3 TABLESPOONS GRANULATED SUGAR

2 TABLESPOONS CORNSTARCH

1 TEASPOON INSTANT ESPRESSO-COFFEE POWDER

1 CUP MILK

5 SQUARES (5 OUNCES) UNSWEETENED CHOCOLATE, CHOPPED

3 TABLESPOONS BUTTER OR MARGARINE, SOFTENED

4 LARGE EGGS, SEPARATED

2 TEASPOONS VANILLA EXTRACT

2 LARGE EGG WHITES

¼ TEASPOON SALT

CONFECTIONERS' SUGAR

1   In 3-quart saucepan, combine 1¼ cups granulated sugar, cornstarch, and espresso powder. With wire whisk, gradually stir in milk until blended. Cook over medium heat, stirring constantly, until mixture has thickened and boils; boil, stirring, 1 minute. Remove from heat.

2   Stir in chocolate and butter until melted and smooth. With whisk, beat in egg yolks until well blended; stir in vanilla. Cool to lukewarm, stirring constantly.

3   Meanwhile, preheat oven to 350°F. Grease eight 6-ounce custard cups or ramekins; sprinkle lightly with remaining 3 tablespoons granulated sugar.

4   In large bowl, with mixer at high speed, beat 6 egg whites and salt just until stiff peaks form when beaters are lifted. Gently fold one-third of beaten egg whites into chocolate mixture; fold back into remaining egg whites just until blended.

5   Spoon into prepared custard cups. Place cups in jelly-roll pan for easier handling. Bake until soufflés have puffed and centers are glossy, 25 to 30 minutes. Dust with confectioners' sugar. Serve immediately.

EACH SOUFFLÉ: ABOUT 355 CALORIES | 7G PROTEIN | 44G CARBOHYDRATE | 19G TOTAL FAT (10G SATURATED) | 3G FIBER | 122MG CHOLESTEROL | 178MG SODIUM

AMARETTO-CHOCOLATE SOUFFLÉ

This irresistibly rich dessert is the kind of sublime treat you'd expect to find on the menu at an upscale restaurant—and you don't have to make a reservation to enjoy it!.

ACTIVE TIME: 20 MINUTES · TOTAL TIME: 1 HOUR

MAKES: 10 SERVINGS

¼ CUP ALL-PURPOSE FLOUR

1 CUP PLUS 2 TABLESPOONS GRANULATED SUGAR

1 TEASPOON INSTANT ESPRESSO-COFFEE POWDER

1 CUP MILK

5 SQUARES (5 OUNCES) UNSWEETENED CHOCOLATE, COARSELY CHOPPED

3 TABLESPOONS BUTTER OR MARGARINE

4 LARGE EGGS, SEPARATED

3 TABLESPOONS ALMOND-FLAVORED LIQUEUR

2 TEASPOONS VANILLA EXTRACT

2 LARGE EGG WHITES

¼ TEASPOON SALT

CONFECTIONERS' SUGAR

1 In 3-quart saucepan, combine flour, ½ cup granulated sugar, and espresso powder. With wire whisk, gradually stir in milk until blended. Cook over medium heat, stirring constantly, until mixture has thickened and boils; boil, stirring, 1 minute. Remove from heat.

2 Stir in chocolate and butter. With whisk, beat in egg yolks until well blended; stir in liqueur and vanilla. Cool to lukewarm, stirring occasionally.

3 Meanwhile, preheat oven to 350°F. Grease 2-quart soufflé dish; sprinkle with 2 tablespoons granulated sugar.

4 In large bowl, with mixer at high speed, beat 6 egg whites and salt until foamy. Sprinkle in remaining ½ cup granulated sugar, 2 tablespoons at a time, beating until sugar has dissolved and egg whites stand in stiff, glossy peaks when beaters are lifted. Gently fold two-thirds of beaten egg whites, in three additions, into chocolate mixture, just until blended. Fold chocolate mixture back into remaining whites, just until blended.

5 Pour chocolate mixture into prepared soufflé dish. Bake until puffed, about 40 minutes. Dust with confectioners' sugar. Serve soufflé immediately.

EACH SERVING: ABOUT 270 CALORIES | 6G PROTEIN | 33G CARBOHYDRATE | 14G TOTAL FAT (8G SATURATED) | 3G FIBER | 97MG CHOLESTEROL | 144MG SODIUM

SOUFFLÉ SECRETS

If you've never made a soufflé before, you may want to try one for
"private consumption" before attempting one for company. Some
pointers: Beat the egg whites until stiff but not dry. Fold the egg
whites into the soufflé base quickly but gently, so as not to deflate
the beaten whites. Be sure to use a straight-sided baking dish for
maxium height. Get the soufflé to the table quickly! To serve, insert
two serving forks, back-to-back, into the center. Gently divide the
soufflé into portions, then scoop them out with a large spoon.

CHOCOLATE PUDDING

Retro food at its best—and who doesn't love chocolate pudding?
This treat has only 2 grams of fat per serving and tastes divine warm
or chilled.

ACTIVE TIME: 5 MINUTES · TOTAL TIME: 10 MINUTES
MAKES: 4 SERVINGS

⅓ CUP SUGAR

¼ CUP CORNSTARCH

3 TABLESPOONS UNSWEETENED COCOA

PINCH SALT

2 CUPS FAT-FREE MILK

1 SQUARE (1 OUNCE) SEMISWEET
CHOCOLATE, FINELY CHOPPED

1 TEASPOON VANILLA EXTRACT

1 In 2-quart saucepan, with wire whisk, mix sugar, cornstarch, cocoa, and
salt until combined. Whisk in milk until blended. Heat mixture to boiling
over medium heat, stirring constantly. Add chocolate; cook 1 minute, stirring, until chocolate has melted and pudding thickens slightly. Remove from
heat; stir in vanilla.

2 Spoon pudding into custard cups. Serve warm or place plastic wrap
directly on surface of pudding and refrigerate to serve cold later.

EACH SERVING: ABOUT 180 CALORIES | 5G PROTEIN | 37G CARBOHYDRATE | 2G TOTAL FAT
(0G SATURATED) | 1G FIBER | 2MG CHOLESTEROL | 105MG SODIUM

QUICK CHOCOLATE PUDDING CAKE

Pudding cake is easy to prepare, especially when the recipe includes buttermilk baking mix, as does ours. This dessert is best eaten warm and is especially fabulous topped with a dollop of whipped cream. If you like, use a vegetable peeler to shave chocolate over the cream (page 166).

ACTIVE TIME: 10 MINUTES · TOTAL TIME: 40 MINUTES PLUS COOLING

MAKES: 6 SERVINGS

---

1   CUP ALL-PURPOSE BUTTERMILK BAKING MIX

¾   UNSWEETENED COCOA

⅓   CUP GRANULATED SUGAR

¼   CUP PACKED BROWN SUGAR

4   TABLESPOONS BUTTER OR MARGARINE

½   CUP MILK

1   TEASPOON VANILLA EXTRACT

1¾ CUPS BOILING WATER

WHIPPED CREAM (OPTIONAL)

1   Preheat oven to 350°F. In medium bowl, combine baking mix, ½ cup cocoa, and granulated sugar. In small bowl, combine brown sugar and remaining ¼ cup cocoa.

2   In small microwave-safe bowl, heat butter in microwave oven on High 45 seconds, or just until butter melts, stirring once. Stir butter, milk, and vanilla into baking mix mixture until blended. Pour batter into ungreased 8-inch square baking dish. Sprinkle evenly with brown-sugar mixture. Pour boiling water evenly over mixture in baking dish. Bake 30 minutes (batter will separate into cake and pudding layers). Cool in pan on wire rack 5 minutes. Serve warm with whipped cream, if you like.

EACH SERVING: ABOUT 265 CALORIES | 4G PROTEIN | 39G CARBOHYDRATE | 13G TOTAL FAT (7G SATURATED) | 4G FIBER | 23MG CHOLESTEROL | 360MG SODIUM

BROWNIE PUDDING CAKE

Two desserts for the price of one! It separates during baking into a fudgy brownie on top of a silky chocolate pudding.

ACTIVE TIME: 20 MINUTES · TOTAL TIME: 50 MINUTES PLUS COOLING

MAKES: 8 SERVINGS

---

2   TEASPOONS INSTANT COFFEE POWDER (OPTIONAL)

2   TABLESPOONS (OPTIONAL) PLUS 1¾ CUPS BOILING WATER

1   CUP ALL-PURPOSE FLOUR

¾   CUP UNSWEETENED COCOA

½   CUP GRANULATED SUGAR

2   TEASPOONS BAKING POWDER

¼   TEASPOON SALT

½   CUP MILK

4   TABLESPOONS BUTTER OR MARGARINE, MELTED

1   TEASPOON VANILLA EXTRACT

½   CUP PACKED BROWN SUGAR

WHIPPED CREAM OR VANILLA ICE CREAM (OPTIONAL)

1   Preheat oven to 350°F. In cup, dissolve coffee powder in 2 tablespoons boiling water, if using.

2   In large bowl, combine flour, ½ cup cocoa, granulated sugar, baking powder, and salt. In measuring cup, combine milk, melted butter, vanilla, and coffee, if using. With wooden spoon, stir milk mixture into flour mixture until just blended. Pour into ungreased 8-inch square baking dish.

3   In small bowl, thoroughly combine brown sugar and remaining ¼ cup cocoa; sprinkle evenly over batter. Carefully pour remaining 1¾ cups boiling water evenly over mixture in baking dish; do not stir.

4   Bake 30 minutes (batter will separate into cake and pudding layers). Cool in pan on wire rack 10 minutes. Serve hot with whipped cream or ice cream, if you like.

EACH SERVING: ABOUT 240 CALORIES | 4G PROTEIN | 43G CARBOHYDRATE | 7G TOTAL FAT (5G SATURATED) | 3G FIBER | 18MG CHOLESTEROL | 267MG SODIUM

BAKED CHOCOLATE-HAZELNUT PUDDINGS

Bake this rich soufflélike dessert in individual ramekins. If you like, substitute toasted blanched almonds for the hazelnuts.

ACTIVE TIME: 30 MINUTES · TOTAL TIME: 55 MINUTES PLUS CHILLING AND COOLING
MAKES: 8 SERVINGS

¾ CUP HAZELNUTS (FILBERTS), TOASTED AND SKINNED (PAGE 93)

¾ CUP SUGAR

4 TABLESPOONS BUTTER OR MARGARINE, SOFTENED

7 LARGE EGGS, SEPARATED

8 SQUARES (8 OUNCES) SEMISWEET CHOCOLATE, MELTED AND COOLED

¼ TEASPOON SALT

¾ CUP HEAVY OR WHIPPING CREAM

1 TEASPOON VANILLA EXTRACT

1 Generously butter eight 6-ounce ramekins.

2 In food processor with knife blade attached, pulse hazelnuts with ¼ cup sugar until finely ground.

3 In large bowl, with mixer at medium speed, beat butter until smooth. Add ¼ cup sugar; beat until creamy. Add egg yolks, one at a time, beating well after each addition. Beat in nut mixture and chocolate until blended.

4 In another large bowl, with mixer at high speed, beat egg whites and salt until soft peaks form when beaters are lifted. Sprinkle in remaining ¼ cup sugar, 2 tablespoons at a time, beating until sugar has dissolved and egg whites stand in stiff, glossy peaks when beaters are lifted. Stir one-fourth of beaten whites into chocolate mixture until well combined. Gently fold remaining whites into chocolate mixture just until blended. Spoon batter into prepared ramekins. Cover and refrigerate 4 hours or up to overnight.

5 Meanwhile, preheat oven to 350°F. Place ramekins in large roasting pan; place pan in oven. Pour enough boiling water into roasting pan to come halfway up sides of ramekins. Bake until knife blade inserted in center comes out with some fudgy batter clinging, about 25 minutes. Transfer ramekins to wire rack to cool 5 minutes.

6 Meanwhile, in small bowl, with mixer at medium speed, beat cream and vanilla until soft peaks form.

7 To serve, scoop out small amount of pudding from top of each dessert; fill with some whipped cream. Replace scooped-out pudding.

EACH SERVING: ABOUT 500 CALORIES | 10G PROTEIN | 37G CARBOHYDRATE | 37G TOTAL FAT
(17G SATURATED) | 3G FIBER | 235MG CHOLESTEROL | 215MG SODIUM

CHOCOLATE STICKY TOFFEE PUDDING

This classic British sweet is enjoying a resurgence in popularity. We devised a chocolate version of this moist, puddinglike cake—and didn't skimp on the heavenly caramel topping.

ACTIVE TIME: 30 MINUTES · TOTAL TIME: 50 MINUTES PLUS STANDING AND COOLING
MAKES: 12 SERVINGS

¾	CUP WATER	5	TABLESPOONS BUTTER OR MARGARINE, SOFTENED
½	CUP CHOPPED PITTED DATES		
1	TEASPOON INSTANT-COFFEE POWDER OR GRANULES	½	CUP GRANULATED SUGAR
		1	LARGE EGG
½	TEASPOON BAKING SODA	½	TEASPOON VANILLA EXTRACT
½	CUP ALL-PURPOSE FLOUR	½	CUP PACKED LIGHT BROWN SUGAR
⅓	CUP UNSWEETENED COCOA	2	TABLESPOONS HEAVY OR WHIPPING CREAM
½	TEASPOON BAKING POWDER		
¼	TEASPOON SALT		WHIPPED CREAM (OPTIONAL)

1 Preheat oven to 350°F. Grease 8-inch square baking pan.

2 In 1-quart saucepan, heat water to boiling over high heat. Remove from heat; stir in dates, instant coffee, and baking soda. Let stand 15 minutes.

3 Meanwhile, in small bowl, combine flour, cocoa, baking powder, and salt. In large bowl, with mixer at medium-high speed, beat 3 tablespoons butter and granulated sugar until creamy. Add egg and vanilla; beat until blended. Reduce speed to low. Alternately add flour mixture and date mixture, beginning and ending with flour mixture; beat just until batter is blended, occasionally scraping bowl with rubber spatula (batter will be thin).

4 Pour batter into prepared pan; spread evenly. Bake until toothpick inserted in center comes out clean, 18 to 20 minutes.

5 Meanwhile, in clean 1-quart saucepan, combine brown sugar, cream, and remaining 2 tablespoons butter; heat to boiling over medium heat, stirring frequently. Boil 1 minute, stirring. Remove from heat.

6 Remove pudding from oven and turn oven control to broil. Pour brown-sugar mixture over hot pudding; spread evenly. Return pudding to oven; broil at closest position to heat source until bubbly, about 30 seconds. Cool in pan on wire rack 15 minutes. Serve warm with whipped cream, if you like.

EACH SERVING: ABOUT 170 CALORIES | 2G PROTEIN | 28G CARBOHYDRATE | 6G TOTAL FAT (4G SATURATED) | 1G FIBER | 34MG CHOLESTEROL | 175MG SODIUM

CHOCOLATE BREAD PUDDING

For this pudding, cubes of bread are steeped in chocolate custard and then layered with ribbons of melted semisweet chocolate.

ACTIVE TIME: 25 MINUTES · TOTAL TIME: 1 HOUR 15 MINUTES PLUS COOLING
MAKES: 8 SERVINGS

---

8   SLICES STALE FIRM WHITE BREAD, CUT INTO 1-INCH PIECES

3   TABLESPOONS PLUS ⅓ CUP SUGAR

8   SQUARES (8 OUNCES) SEMISWEET CHOCOLATE, MELTED

3   CUPS MILK

3   LARGE EGGS

1½ TEASPOONS VANILLA EXTRACT

1   Grease 8-inch square baking dish. Scatter one-third of bread pieces in prepared dish in even layer; sprinkle with 1 tablespoon sugar and drizzle with 2 tablespoons melted chocolate. Repeat layers. Top with remaining bread pieces. Set remaining chocolate aside.

2   In 2-quart saucepan, heat milk to simmering over medium-high heat.

3   Meanwhile, in medium bowl, with wire whisk, combine eggs and ⅓ cup sugar. Whisking constantly, slowly pour simmering milk into egg mixture. Stir in remaining melted chocolate and vanilla.

4   Pour egg mixture over bread. Refrigerate until bread has absorbed chocolate mixture, about 3 hours, gently stirring mixture occasionally.

5   Meanwhile, preheat oven to 325°F. Sprinkle pudding with remaining 1 tablespoon sugar. Place dish in medium roasting pan; place in oven. Carefully pour enough boiling water into roasting pan to come halfway up sides of dish. Bake until knife inserted in center of pudding comes out clean, about 50 minutes. Remove dish from roasting pan. Place on wire rack to cool 15 minutes. Serve pudding warm, or cover and refrigerate to serve cold later.

TIP Firm white bread is used for most of our bread puddings. Excellent options are French or Italian bread, challah, brioche, and raisin bread. If you're buying sliced bread in the supermarket, look for one with dense texture. Labels like "hearty," "traditional," and "brick oven-baked" are cues to good texture. The bread need not be fresh; in fact, slightly stale bread is preferable.

EACH SERVING: ABOUT 355 CALORIES | 9G PROTEIN | 49G CARBOHYDRATE | 15G TOTAL FAT (8G SATURATED) | 3G FIBER | 93MG CHOLESTEROL | 225MG SODIUM

CHOCOLATE-CHERRY BREAD PUDDING

Perfect for chocoholics in search of some good old-fashioned comfort food. This pudding is delicious as is, but it is even better when served with softly whipped cream flavored with a splash of kirsch or vanilla.

ACTIVE TIME: 20 MINUTES · TOTAL TIME: 1 HOUR 15 MINUTES PLUS STANDING AND COOLING
MAKES: 8 SERVINGS

3½ CUPS MILK

4 SQUARES (4 OUNCES) SEMISWEET CHOCOLATE

2 SQUARES (2 OUNCES) UNSWEETENED CHOCOLATE

½ CUP SUGAR

2 TEASPOONS VANILLA EXTRACT

½ TEASPOON SALT

3 LARGE EGGS

8 OUNCES (ABOUT 10 SLICES) STALE FIRM WHITE BREAD, CUT INTO ¼-INCH PIECES

½ CUP DRIED TART CHERRIES

1 Grease 8-inch square baking dish. In 2-quart saucepan, heat milk to simmering over medium-high heat.

2 Meanwhile, in 3-quart saucepan, melt semisweet and unsweetened chocolates over low heat, stirring frequently, until smooth. Remove from heat. With wire whisk, stir in sugar, vanilla, and salt. Stir in eggs until combined. Slowly whisk simmering milk into melted-chocolate mixture until blended. Gently stir in bread. Let stand 20 minutes to allow bread to absorb milk mixture, stirring once.

3 Meanwhile, preheat oven to 325°F. Pour bread mixture into prepared baking dish; sprinkle with cherries. Cover with foil and bake 40 minutes. Uncover and bake until knife inserted in center of pudding comes out almost clean, about 15 minutes longer. Cool in pan on wire rack 20 minutes to serve warm, or cover and refrigerate to serve cold later.

EACH SERVING: ABOUT 350 CALORIES | 10G PROTEIN | 48G CARBOHYDRATE | 15G TOTAL FAT (8G SATURATED) | 5G FIBER | 95MG CHOLESTEROL | 375MG SODIUM

CHOCOLATE PÔTS DE CRÈME

These rich chocolate custards are the perfect ending to an elegant dinner. They can be prepared several hours ahead or even the day before. For a fancy presentation, top each serving with a whipped cream rosette and a chocolate-covered coffee bean, candied rose or violet, or fat chocolate curl.

ACTIVE TIME: 15 MINUTES · TOTAL TIME: 45 MINUTES PLUS CHILLING AND COOLING
MAKES: 6 SERVINGS

3   SQUARES (3 OUNCES) SEMISWEET CHOCOLATE, CHOPPED

2½ CUPS MILK

2   LARGE EGGS

2   LARGE EGG YOLKS

¼   CUP SUGAR

1   TEASPOON VANILLA EXTRACT

1   Preheat oven to 350°F. In 3-quart saucepan, heat chocolate and ¼ cup milk over low heat, stirring frequently, until chocolate has melted and mixture is smooth; remove from heat.

2   In 2-quart saucepan, heat remaining 2¼ cups milk to boiling over medium-high heat; stir into chocolate mixture until blended. In large bowl, whisk eggs, egg yolks, sugar, and vanilla until well blended. Gradually whisk in chocolate mixture until well combined. Pour into six 6-ounce ramekins or custard cups.

3   Place ramekins in medium roasting pan; place in oven. Carefully pour enough boiling water into roasting pan to come halfway up sides of ramekins. Cover roasting pan with foil, crimping edges loosely. Bake custards until knife inserted halfway between edge and center of custard comes out clean, 30 to 35 minutes. Remove foil; transfer ramekins to wire rack to cool. Refrigerate until well chilled, about 3 hours.

EACH SERVING: ABOUT 210 CALORIES | 7G PROTEIN | 22G CARBOHYDRATE | 11G TOTAL FAT (6G SATURATED) | 1G FIBER | 156MG CHOLESTEROL | 75MG SODIUM

CHOCOLATE FONDUE WITH FRUIT

Dipping succulent chunks of fresh fruit into a rich chocolate sauce is a delicious way to end a meal with friends. We suggest using bananas, pears, and strawberries, but almost any in-season fruit will do. During the summer, use apricots, peaches, or nectarines, and in the fall choose a variety of apples: sweet, tart, and something in between.

ACTIVE TIME: 15 MINUTES · TOTAL TIME: 20 MINUTES

MAKES: 8 SERVINGS

6	SQUARES (6 OUNCES) SEMISWEET CHOCOLATE, COARSELY CHOPPED	2	TO 3 SMALL PEARS, CORED AND CUT INTO ½-INCH-THICK WEDGES
½	CUP HALF-AND-HALF OR LIGHT CREAM	1	PINT STRAWBERRIES, HULLED
½	TEASPOON VANILLA EXTRACT	½	CUP FINELY CHOPPED TOASTED ALMONDS (PAGE 93)
4	SMALL BANANAS, PEELED AND CUT INTO ½-INCH-THICK SLICES		

1 In 1-quart saucepan, heat chocolate and half-and-half over low heat, stirring frequently, until chocolate has melted and mixture is smooth, about 5 minutes. Stir in vanilla; keep warm.

2 To serve, arrange bananas, pears, and strawberries on large platter. Spoon sauce into small bowl; place nuts in separate small bowl. With forks or toothpicks, have guests dip fruit into chocolate sauce, then into nuts.

EACH SERVING: ABOUT 250 CALORIES | 4G PROTEIN | 36G CARBOHYDRATE | 13G TOTAL FAT (5G SATURATED) | 6G FIBER | 6MG CHOLESTEROL | 10MG SODIUM

CHOCOLATE ÉCLAIRS

Why buy éclairs? Nothing can compare to your first bite of a freshly prepared éclair made right at home.

ACTIVE TIME: 1 HOUR

TOTAL TIME: 1 HOUR 40 MINUTES PLUS CHILLING, COOLING, AND STANDING

MAKES: 30 ÉCLAIRS

CHOCOLATE PASTRY CREAM

2¼ CUPS MILK

3 SQUARES (3 OUNCES) SEMISWEET CHOCOLATE, CHOPPED

1 SQUARES (1 OUNCE) UNSWEETENED CHOCOLATE, CHOPPED

4 LARGE EGG YOLKS

⅔ CUP SUGAR

¼ CUP ALL-PURPOSE FLOUR

¼ CUP CORNSTARCH

1 TABLESPOON VANILLA EXTRACT

CHOUX PASTRY

½ CUP BUTTER OR MARGARINE (1 STICK), CUT INTO PIECES

1 CUP WATER

¼ TEASPOON SALT

1 CUP ALL-PURPOSE FLOUR

4 LARGE EGGS

CHOCOLATE GLAZE

3 SQUARES (3 OUNCES) SEMISWEET CHOCOLATE, CHOPPED

3 TABLESPOONS HEAVY OR WHIPPING CREAM

1   Prepare Chocolate Pastry Cream: In 3-quart saucepan, heat 2 cups milk over medium-high heat until bubbles form around edge.

2   In 1-quart saucepan, melt semisweet and unsweetened chocolates, stirring frequently, until smooth. Meanwhile, in large bowl, with wire whisk, beat egg yolks, remaining ¼ cup milk, and sugar until combined; whisk in flour and cornstarch until blended. Gradually whisk hot milk into egg-yolk mixture. Return milk mixture to saucepan; cook over medium-high heat, whisking constantly, until mixture has thickened and boils. Reduce heat to low and cook, stirring, 2 minutes.

3   Remove from heat; stir in melted chocolate and vanilla until blended. Pour pastry cream into shallow dish. Press plastic wrap directly onto surface. Refrigerate until cool, at least 2 hours or up to overnight.

4   Preheat oven to 400°F. Grease and flour large cookie sheet.

5   Prepare Choux Pastry: In 3-quart saucepan, combine butter, water, and salt; heat over medium-high heat until butter has melted and mixture boils. Remove from heat. Add flour all at once; with wooden spoon, vigorously stir until mixture leaves side of pan and forms a ball. Add eggs to flour mixture, one at a time, beating well after each addition, until mixture is smooth and satiny. (For tips, see Choux Pastry, opposite.)

CHOUX PASTRY

Choux pastry dough is unique because it is cooked twice: first on the stove and then in the oven. The dough makes a light, airy, hollow pastry that is perfect for filling with ice cream, whipped cream, or pastry cream.

• When cooking the dough, be sure the butter is completely melted by the time the water comes to a full boil. If too much water evaporates, the dough will be dry.

• For the highest puff, always shape and bake choux pastry dough while it's still warm.

• Bake the pastries until golden brown: Pale, undercooked pastries collapse when removed from the oven.

• Choux dough creates a lot of steam when baked: This steam needs to be released or the pastries will become soggy. As soon as the pastries are removed from the oven, use the tip of a small knife to cut a slit into the side of each one.

• Unfilled choux dough pastries can be frozen in heavy-duty zip-tight plastic bags for up to one month; simply crisp in a 400°F oven for a few minutes before serving.

6   Spoon dough into large pastry bag fitted with ½-inch plain tip. Pipe dough in lengths about 3½ inches long and ¾ inch wide, 1 inch apart, on prepared cookie sheet to make about 30 éclairs. With moistened finger, gently smooth tops.

7   Bake until golden, about 40 minutes. Remove éclairs from oven and turn it off; with tip of knife, make small slit in end of each éclair to release steam. Return éclairs to oven; let stand 10 minutes. Transfer éclairs to wire racks to cool completely.

8   With small knife, make hole in one end of each éclair. Whisk pastry cream until smooth; spoon into clean large pastry bag fitted with ¼-inch plain tip. Pipe pastry cream into éclairs.

9   Prepare Chocolate Glaze: In 6-inch skillet or 1-quart saucepan, combine chocolate and cream; heat over low heat, stirring frequently, until chocolate has melted and mixture is smooth. Remove from heat. Dip top of each éclair into chocolate mixture, smoothing with small metal spatula if necessary. Let stand on wire racks until chocolate sets.

EACH SERVING: ABOUT 115 CALORIES | 3G PROTEIN | 12G CARBOHYDRATE | 6G TOTAL FAT (4G SATURATED) | 1G FIBER | 70MG CHOLESTEROL | 70MG SODIUM

CHOCOLATE ICE CREAM

This ice cream is truly an intense eating experience, thanks to a generous amount of unsweetened and semisweet chocolates and its very rich vanilla ice-cream base.

ACTIVE TIME: 10 MINUTES · TOTAL TIME: 30 MINUTES PLUS CHILLING AND FREEZING
MAKES: 6 CUPS OR 12 SERVINGS

3   CUPS HALF-AND-HALF OR LIGHT CREAM

4   LARGE EGG YOLKS

¾   CUP SUGAR

⅛   TEASPOON SALT

1   CUP HEAVY OR WHIPPING CREAM

1   TEASPOON VANILLA EXTRACT

3   SQUARES (3 OUNCES) UNSWEETENED CHOCOLATE, CHOPPED

2   SQUARES (2 OUNCES) SEMISWEET CHOCOLATE, CHOPPED

1   In heavy 3-quart saucepan, heat half-and-half to boiling over medium-high heat.

2   Meanwhile, in medium bowl, with wire whisk, whisk egg yolks, sugar, and salt until smooth. Gradually whisk half-and-half into egg-yolk mixture. Return mixture to saucepan; cook over medium heat, stirring constantly, just until mixture coats back of spoon (do not boil, or it will curdle). Remove from heat. Strain custard through sieve into large bowl; add ¾ cup heavy cream and vanilla.

3   In heavy 2-quart saucepan, melt unsweetened and semisweet chocolates with remaining ¼ cup cream over low heat, stirring frequently, until smooth. Stir 1 cup vanilla mixture into chocolate mixture; stir back into vanilla mixture. Press plastic wrap onto surface of custard. Refrigerate until well chilled, at least 2 hours or up to overnight.

4   Freeze in ice-cream maker as manufacturer directs.

EACH SERVING: ABOUT 275 CALORIES | 4G PROTEIN | 21G CARBOHYDRATE | 21G TOTAL FAT (13G SATURATED) | 2G FIBER | 120MG CHOLESTEROL | 61MG SODIUM

CHOCOLATE SORBET

When you want a frozen chocolate dessert that is a bit lighter than ice cream, sorbet is a good choice. This one packs plenty of satisfying chocolate flavor.

ACTIVE TIME: 10 MINUTES · TOTAL TIME: 20 MINUTES PLUS CHILLING AND FREEZING
MAKES: 4 CUPS OR 8 SERVINGS

¾ CUP SUGAR

2½ CUPS WATER

2 SQUARES (2 OUNCES) UNSWEETENED CHOCOLATE, CHOPPED

¼ CUP LIGHT CORN SYRUP

1½ TEASPOONS VANILLA EXTRACT

1   In 2-quart saucepan, combine sugar and water; heat to boiling over high heat, stirring until sugar has dissolved. Reduce heat to medium; cook 3 minutes. Remove from heat.

2   In heavy 1-quart saucepan, heat chocolate and corn syrup over low heat, stirring frequently, until chocolate has melted and mixture is smooth.

3   With wire whisk, stir 1 cup sugar syrup into chocolate mixture until well blended. Stir chocolate mixture into remaining sugar syrup in saucepan; stir in vanilla. Pour into medium bowl; cover and refrigerate until well chilled, about 1½ hours.

4   Freeze in ice-cream maker as manufacturer directs.

EACH SERVING: ABOUT 140 CALORIES | 1G PROTEIN | 29G CARBOHYDRATE | 4G TOTAL FAT (2G SATURATED) | 1G FIBER | 0MG CHOLESTEROL | 14MG SODIUM

BROWNIE SUNDAE CUPS

What could be better than brownie cupcakes filled with scoops of vanilla ice cream and drizzled with fudge sauce? Both the brownies and sauce can be prepared hours ahead. Assemble the sundaes just before serving.

ACTIVE TIME: 20 MINUTES · **TOTAL TIME:** 50 MINUTES PLUS COOLING
MAKES: 6 SERVINGS

BROWNIE CUPS

1	CUP ALL-PURPOSE FLOUR
½	CUP UNSWEETENED COCOA
1	TEASPOON BAKING POWDER
¼	TEASPOON SALT
¾	CUP BUTTER OR MARGARINE (1½ STICKS)
1½	CUPS SUGAR
3	LARGE EGGS
2	TEASPOONS VANILLA EXTRACT

HOT FUDGE SAUCE

½	CUP SUGAR
⅓	CUP UNSWEETENED COCOA
¼	CUP HEAVY OR WHIPPING CREAM
2	TABLESPOONS BUTTER OR MARGARINE, CUT IN PIECES
1	TEASPOON VANILLA EXTRACT

1 PINT VANILLA ICE CREAM

1   Preheat oven to 350°F. Grease 6 jumbo muffin-pan cups (about 4" by 2" each) or six 6-ounce custard cups.

2   Prepare cups: In medium bowl, combine flour, cocoa, baking powder, and salt. In 3-quart saucepan, melt butter over medium-low heat. Remove from heat; stir in sugar. Add eggs and vanilla; stir until well mixed. Stir in flour mixture just until blended. Spoon batter evenly into prepared cups.

3   Bake until toothpick inserted in center comes out almost clean, 30 to 35 minutes. Cool in pan on wire rack 5 minutes. Run tip of thin knife around brownies to loosen from sides of pan. Invert brownies onto rack; cool 10 minutes longer to serve warm, or cool completely to serve later.

4   While cups are cooling, prepare sauce: In heavy 1-quart saucepan, combine sugar, cocoa, cream, and butter; heat to boiling over medium-high heat, stirring frequently. Remove from heat; stir in vanilla. Serve sauce warm, or cool completely, then cover and refrigerate up to 2 weeks. Gently reheat before using. (Makes about ⅔ cup.)

5   Assemble sundaes: With small knife, cut 1½- to 2-inch circle in center of each brownie; remove tops and set aside. Scoop out brownie centers, making sure not to cut through bottoms of brownies. Transfer brownie

centers to small bowl; reserve to sprinkle over ice cream another day. Place each brownie cup on dessert plate. Scoop ice cream into brownie cups and drizzle with hot fudge sauce; replace brownie tops.

EACH SERVING WITHOUT SAUCE: ABOUT 500 CALORIES | 7G PROTEIN | 61G CARBOHYDRATE | 28G TOTAL FAT (16G SATURATED) | 3G FIBER | 152MG CHOLESTEROL | 355MG SODIUM

EACH TABLESPOON FUDGE SAUCE: ABOUT 80 CALORIES | 1G PROTEIN | 10G CARBOHYDRATE | 5G TOTAL FAT (3G SATURATED) | 1G FIBER | 14MG CHOLESTEROL | 25MG SODIUM

ROCKY ROAD ICE CREAM CAKE

This ooey-gooey treat is like a big sundae made in a springform pan. If you run short on time, jarred fudge sauce will do just fine.

ACTIVE TIME: 30 MINUTES · TOTAL TIME: 40 MINUTES PLUS CHILLING AND FREEZING
MAKES: 14 SERVINGS

FUDGE SAUCE

1   CUP HEAVY OR WHIPPING CREAM

¾   CUP SUGAR

4   SQUARES (4 OUNCES) UNSWEETENED CHOCOLATE, CHOPPED

2   TABLESPOONS LIGHT CORN SYRUP

2   TABLESPOONS BUTTER OR MARGARINE

2   TEASPOONS VANILLA EXTRACT

ROCKY ROAD CAKE

2   PINTS CHOCOLATE ICE CREAM, SOFTENED

14 CHOCOLATE SANDWICH COOKIES

2   CUPS MINIATURE MARSHMALLOWS

1   CUP SALTED PEANUTS, COARSELY CHOPPED

1   Prepare Fudge Sauce: In heavy 2-quart saucepan, combine cream, sugar, chocolate, and corn syrup. Heat to boiling over medium heat, stirring occasionally. Cook over medium-low heat, stirring constantly, until sauce thickens slightly, 4 minutes longer. Remove from heat. Add butter and vanilla; stir until butter has melted and sauce is smooth and glossy. Cover surface of sauce with plastic wrap; refrigerate until cool, about 2 hours. Makes about 1⅔ cups.

2   When sauce is cool, assemble Rocky Road Cake: Wrap outside of 9" by 3" springform pan with foil. Spoon 1 pint softened chocolate ice cream into pan. Cover ice cream with plastic wrap; press down to spread ice cream evenly and eliminate air pockets; remove plastic wrap. Insert cookies, upright, into ice cream to form a ring around side of pan, making sure to push cookie to pan bottom. Sprinkle 1 cup marshmallows and ½ cup peanuts over ice cream; gently press in with hand.

3   Spoon remaining ice cream over marshmallows and peanuts. Place plastic wrap on ice cream and spread evenly; remove plastic. Spread ⅔ cup Fudge Sauce over ice cream (if sauce is too firm, microwave briefly to soften but do not reheat); reserve remaining sauce. Sprinkle remaining marshmallows and peanuts over sauce; press in gently with hand. Cover cake with plastic wrap and freeze until firm, at least 6 hours.

4   To serve, uncover cake and remove foil. Wrap towels dampened with warm water around side of pan for about 20 seconds to slightly soften ice cream. Remove side of pan and place cake on cake stand or plate. Let stand at room temperature about 10 minutes for easier slicing. Meanwhile, if you wish to serve hot sauce to spoon over cake, place remaining Fudge Sauce in microwave-safe bowl. Heat in microwave oven, uncovered, on High 30 to 40 seconds or until hot, stirring once.

EACH SERVING: ABOUT 365 CALORIES | 7G PROTEIN | 36G CARBOHYDRATE | 23G TOTAL FAT (11G SATURATED) | 3G FIBER | 77MG CHOLESTEROL | 220MG SODIUM

BROWNIE BAKED ALASKA

You'll love our new take on this classic dessert. Vanilla ice cream enriched with cherries and chocolate is layered between fudgy brownies and topped with dark cocoa meringue. You can assemble the ice-cream loaf and freeze it for up to two weeks. About thirty minutes before serving, prepare the meringue, spread it over the frozen loaf, and pop it into the oven until the meringue peaks are lightly browned.

ACTIVE TIME: 55 MINUTES · TOTAL TIME: 1 HOUR 25 MINUTES PLUS COOLING AND FREEZING
MAKES: 12 SERVINGS

BROWNIE LAYERS

6 TABLESPOONS BUTTER OR MARGARINE (¾ STICK)

2 SQUARES (2 OUNCES) UNSWEETENED CHOCOLATE, CHOPPED

2 SQUARES (2 OUNCES) SEMISWEET CHOCOLATE, CHOPPED

¾ CUP GRANULATED SUGAR

1½ TEASPOONS VANILLA EXTRACT

¼ TEASPOON SALT

2 LARGE EGGS

½ CUP ALL-PURPOSE FLOUR

2 PINTS VANILLA ICE CREAM WITH CHERRIES AND FUDGE FLAKES, SOFTENED

COCOA MERINGUE

¼ CUP CONFECTIONERS' SUGAR

¼ CUP UNSWEETENED COCOA

2 TABLESPOONS PLUS 2 TEASPOONS PASTEURIZED POWDERED EGG WHITES (SUCH AS JUST WHITE BRAND)

½ CUP WARM WATER

PINCH SALT

¼ CUP GRANULATED SUGAR

1 Prepare brownie layers: Preheat oven to 350°F. Grease 8-inch square baking pan. Line pan with foil; grease foil and dust with flour.

2 In heavy 2-quart saucepan, melt butter and unsweetened and semisweet chocolates over low heat, stirring frequently, until smooth. Remove from heat. With wooden spoon, stir in granulated sugar, vanilla, and salt. Stir in eggs until well mixed. Stir in flour just until blended. Spread batter evenly in prepared pan.

3 Bake 25 minutes (toothpick inserted in center will not come out clean). Cool completely in pan on wire rack. When cool, invert onto cutting board; peel off foil. Cut brownie in half.

4 Line 8½" by 4½" by 2½" metal loaf pan with plastic wrap. Press one brownie layer into bottom of pan. Spoon ice cream over brownie; spread into a smooth, even layer. Top with remaining brownie. Cover pan with plastic wrap and freeze until firm, at least 4 hours.

5   About 30 minutes before serving, preheat oven to 475°F. Prepare cocoa meringue: In small bowl, sift confectioners' sugar and cocoa. In large bowl, with wire whisk, gently mix powdered egg whites and warm water until mixture is well blended and egg whites have dissolved. Stir in salt. With mixer at medium speed, beat egg whites until frothy. Increase speed to high; sprinkle in granulated sugar, 2 tablespoons at a time, beating until sugar has dissolved and egg whites stand in stiff, glossy peaks when beaters are lifted. With rubber spatula, gently fold cocoa mixture into egg whites, one-third at a time, until evenly blended.

6   Remove plastic wrap from top of loaf. Invert loaf onto oven-safe platter; remove remaining plastic wrap. Spread cocoa meringue over top and sides of loaf, swirling with spatula to form peaks and making sure meringue extends onto dish to completely seal in ice cream and brownie. Bake until meringue peaks are lightly browned, 3 to 4 minutes. Serve immediately.

EACH SERVING: ABOUT 385 CALORIES | 8G PROTEIN | 45G CARBOHYDRATE | 21G TOTAL FAT (14G SATURATED) | 3G FIBER | 98MG CHOLESTEROL | 187MG SODIUM

FINISHING TOUCHES

When what you are craving is just a little something sweet, this is the chapter to turn to. It is filled with chocolaty treats: easy-to-prepare hot and cold beverages, decadent sauces, and beautiful garnishes.

COCOA TIME Is there anything better on a cold winter's day than a favorite mug filled with steaming hot chocolate and topped with a fluff of whipped cream? Or anything more refreshing on an August afternoon than a frosty glass of iced cappuccino dusted with fragrant cinnamon? Recipes for these concoctions plus a convenient homemade cocoa mix are all supplied here.

FAVORITE FUDGE SAUCE A bowl of ice cream is always a treat, but top it with one of our sauces and it becomes an experience. Rich, velvety—you will want to keep a spare batch in the refrigerator. Spoon it over a wedge of pound cake and smother with strawberries, or use it to top a classic banana split.

CHOCOLATE GARNISHES After preparing a fabulous chocolate dessert, why not top it off with a beautiful chocolate embellishment, such as chocolate curls, wedges, ruffles, or even butterflies. Our step-by-step instructions make it easy. All of the garnishes can be prepared at least a week ahead and then stored between layers of waxed paper in an airtight container in the refrigerator.

Stencils (page 170)

HOT CHOCOLATE

Here's a hot chocolate to savor with every sip. For a sophisticated varia-
tion, add ¼ cup orange or raspberry liqueur just before serving.

TOTAL TIME: 10 MINUTES

MAKES: 4 CUPS OR 6 SERVINGS

WHIPPED CREAM

1   CUP HEAVY OR WHIPPING CREAM

2   TABLESPOONS CONFECTIONERS'
    SUGAR

2   TEASPOONS VANILLA EXTRACT

HOT CHOCOLATE

6   SQUARES (6 OUNCES) SEMISWEET
    CHOCOLATE, CHOPPED

1⅔ CUPS BOILING WATER

1½ CUPS MILK

UNSWEETENED COCOA (OPTIONAL)

1   In small bowl, with mixer at medium speed, beat cream, confectioners'
sugar, and vanilla until stiff peaks form. Cover and refrigerate if not using
right away.

2   Place chocolate in 1-quart saucepan. Pour ⅓ cup boiling water over-
chocolate and stir until chocolate melts. Add milk and remaining 1⅓ cups
boiling water; heat over medium until hot (do not boil), whisking constantly.
Pour into warm mugs and top with whipped cream. Sprinkle with cocoa,
if desired.

EACH SERVING: ABOUT 330 CALORIES | 4G PROTEIN | 22G CARBOHYDRATE | 26G TOTAL FAT
(16G SATURATED) | 2G FIBER | 64MG CHOLESTEROL | 50MG SODIUM

FROSTY CAPPUCCINO

We guarantee that this rich blender drink is better than what you can order at a specialty coffee store. Blend up a batch the next time you need a cooling treat, and accessorize each drink with a straw for easy sipping.

TOTAL TIME: 5 MINUTES

MAKES: 2 SERVINGS

1   CUP LOWFAT (1%) MILK

1   TABLESPOON CHOCOLATE-FLAVORED SYRUP

1   TEASPOON INSTANT ESPRESSO-COFFEE POWDER

2   ICE CUBES

SUGAR (OPTIONAL)

⅛   TEASPOON GROUND CINNAMON

In blender combine milk, chocolate syrup, coffee powder, and ice cubes; blend 1 minute. Pour into two chilled glasses. Add sugar to taste, if you like. Sprinkle with cinnamon.

EACH SERVING: ABOUT 75 CALORIES | 4G PROTEIN | 12G CARBOHYDRATE | 1G TOTAL FAT (1G SATURATED) | 0.5G FIBER | 5MG CHOLESTEROL | 65MG SODIUM

WINTER COCOA MIX

Storing this mixture with the vanilla bean makes for the ultimate cup of cocoa.

TOTAL TIME: 10 MINUTES

MAKES: 3½ CUPS MIX, ENOUGH FOR 18 SERVINGS

1½ CUPS UNSWEETENED COCOA

1¼ CUPS SUGAR

5   SQUARES (5 OUNCES) SEMISWEET CHOCOLATE, COARSELY CHOPPED

1   VANILLA BEAN, CUT CROSSWISE IN HALF, THEN CUT LENGTHWISE IN HALF

In food processor with knife blade attached, combine cocoa, sugar, and chocolate; process until almost smooth. Stir in vanilla-bean pieces. Store powder at room temperature in tightly covered container up to 6 months.

EACH TABLESPOON DRY MIX: ABOUT 35 CALORIES | 1G PROTEIN | 8G CARBOHYDRATE | 1G TOTAL FAT (0G SATURATED) | 1G FIBER | 0MG CHOLESTEROL | 5MG SODIUM

A DELICIOUS SIP OF HISTORY

Chocolate beverages have been prized in Mexico for well over 500 years. In the courts of the Aztec rulers, chocolate was spiked with chiles, herbs, and, occasionally, honey.

Today, most of the chocolate produced in Mexico is still used for beverages—primarily for *chocolate caliente* (hot chocolate). The chocolate itself is sold in grainy-textured disks made from dark-roasted cacao beans that have been heated and ground with sugar, cinnamon, almonds, and vanilla. Look for them in supermarkets, specialty stores, and ethnic groceries.

To prepare Mexican hot chocolate in the authentic manner, break a chocolate disk into a cup or pot of hot milk or hot water. When the chocolate melts, place a *molinillo* (a carved wooden beater with a series of disks at the bottom) into the chocolate mixture and spin it between your palms to whip up a chocolaty froth. If you don't have a *molinillo*, try using a small whisk instead.

HOT DARK CHOCOLATE

Ladurée, a fabulous Parisian pastry shop, serves up the richest and most delicious hot chocolate in the world. Their secret is that they use bittersweet rather than semisweet chocolate, which makes the drink a bit more elegant. If you like, try bittersweet chocolate in this delicious hot chocolate—you won't be disappointed.

ACTIVE TIME: 5 MINUTES · **TOTAL TIME:** 15 MINUTES
MAKES: 4 SERVINGS

1 QUART MILK	2 SQUARES (2 OUNCES) SEMISWEET CHOCOLATE, FINELY CHOPPED
¼ CUP UNSWEETENED COCOA	
¼ CUP SUGAR	2 TEASPOONS VANILLA EXTRACT

1 In 2-quart saucepan, heat milk to simmering over medium heat.
2 With wire whisk, stir in cocoa, sugar, chocolate, and vanilla. Heat mixture, stirring occasionally, until chocolate melts, about 3 minutes. Pour into warm mugs to serve.

EACH SERVING: ABOUT 290 CALORIES | 10G PROTEIN | 34G CARBOHYDRATE | 13G TOTAL FAT (8G SATURATED) | 3G FIBER | 33MG CHOLESTEROL | 120MG SODIUM

COFFEE-SPIKED HOT CHOCOLATE

Prepare as directed, but stir **¼ cup coffee-flavored liqueur** into chocolate mixture just before serving.

EACH SERVING: ABOUT 345 CALORIES | 10G PROTEIN | 40G CARBOHYDRATE | 13G TOTAL FAT (8G SATURATED) | 3G FIBER | 33MG CHOLESTEROL | 120MG SODIUM

MEXICAN HOT CHOCOLATE

Prepare as directed, but add **1 cinnamon stick (3 inches)** to milk in Step 1.

OUR SUBLIME CHOCOLATE SAUCE

You'll want to make a double batch of this! Keep it refrigerated for up to one week, gently reheating only the amount you want to use.

TOTAL TIME: 15 MINUTES

MAKES: 1¾ CUPS

4 SQUARES (4 OUNCES) UNSWEETENED CHOCOLATE, CHOPPED

1 CUP HEAVY OR WHIPPING CREAM

¾ CUP SUGAR

2 TABLESPOONS LIGHT CORN SYRUP

2 TABLESPOONS BUTTER OR MARGARINE

2 TEASPOONS VANILLA EXTRACT

1 In heavy 2-quart saucepan, combine chocolate, cream, sugar, and corn syrup; heat to boiling over high heat, stirring constantly. Reduce heat to medium. Cook at a gentle boil, stirring constantly, until sauce has thickened slightly, about 5 minutes.

2 Remove from heat; stir in butter and vanilla until smooth and glossy. Serve hot, or cool completely, then cover and refrigerate up to 1 week.

EACH SERVING: ABOUT 85 CALORIES | 1G PROTEIN | 8G CARBOHYDRATE | 6G TOTAL FAT (4G SATURATED) | 1G FIBER | 14MG CHOLESTEROL | 14MG SODIUM

HOT FUDGE SAUCE

Use this rich, chocolaty sauce as a topping for ice cream or other desserts. Unsweetened cocoa powder makes it easy to prepare.

TOTAL TIME: 15 MINUTES
MAKES: 1¼ CUPS

¾ CUP SUGAR

½ CUP UNSWEETENED COCOA

½ CUP HEAVY OR WHIPPING CREAM

4 TABLESPOONS BUTTER OR MARGARINE, CUT INTO PIECES

1 TEASPOON VANILLA EXTRACT

In heavy 1-quart saucepan, combine sugar, cocoa, cream, and butter; heat to boiling over high heat, stirring frequently. Remove from heat; stir in vanilla. Serve warm, or cool completely, then cover and refrigerate up to 2 weeks. Gently reheat before using.

EACH TABLESPOON: ABOUT 75 CALORIES | 1G PROTEIN | 9G CARBOHYDRATE | 5G TOTAL FAT (3G SATURATED) | 1G FIBER | 14MG CHOLESTEROL | 26MG SODIUM

CHOCOLATE CURLS

Chocolate curls turn a simple pie or cake into a special dessert. Make a batch and store them in the refrigerator in an airtight container between layers of waxed paper. Use the curls when you want to gussy up a home-made dessert. White chocolate can also be used for curls. Just be very careful when melting it, as it is more delicate than semisweet.

TOTAL TIME: 15 MINUTES PLUS COOLING

1   PACKAGE (6 OUNCES) SEMISWEET
    CHOCOLATE CHIPS

2   TABLESPOONS VEGETABLE
    SHORTENING

1   Line a 5¾" by 3¼" loaf pan with foil. In heavy 1-quart sauce-pan, combine chocolate chips and shortening; melt over low heat, stirring frequently, until smooth.

2   Pour chocolate mixture into prepared pan. Refrigerate until chocolate is set, about 2 hours.

3   Remove chilled chocolate from pan by lifting edges of foil. Using vegetable peeler and working over waxed paper, draw blade across surface of chocolate to make large curls. If chocolate is too cold and curls break, let stand at room temperature until slightly soft-

ened, about 30 minutes. Use toothpick or wooden skewer to transfer curls to dessert for garnish.

CHOCOLATE RUFFLES

If the temperature of the chocolate is just right, the ruffles will fold nicely.

ACTIVE TIME: 20 MINUTES · **TOTAL TIME:** 25 MINUTES PLUS COOLING
MAKES: ENOUGH RUFFLES TO TOP A 9-INCH CAKE

---

8   SQUARES (8 OUNCES) SEMISWEET
    CHOCOLATE, CHOPPED

1   In heavy 1-quart saucepan, melt chocolate over low heat, stirring constantly. Spoon about ¼ cup melted chocolate onto inverted 15½" by 10½" clean jelly-roll pan. With metal spatula, spread chocolate to cover pan bottom evenly. Refrigerate just until chocolate is firm, about 10 minutes.

2   Prepare ruffles: Place chocolate-covered jelly-roll pan, with 10½-inch side toward you, on damp cloth to keep it from moving. With blade of wide spatula, starting at far corner, scrape about a 3-inch-wide strip of chocolate toward you, pulling spatula with one hand and gathering side of chocolate strip with your other hand; allow loose side to fan out. (Consistency of chocolate is very important. If too soft, it will gather into a mush; if too hard, it will break and crumble. Let overfirm chocolate stand at room temperature a few minutes until soft enough to work with; return too-soft chocolate to refrigerator.) Place ruffles on cookie sheet; refrigerate until firm.

3   Continue making ruffles with chocolate on pan. Repeat with remaining melted chocolate, using a clean jelly-roll pan each time. (The more jelly-roll pans you have on hand, the faster you can make ruffles.) If ruffles break while making, return chocolate to saucepan, gently remelt, and try again.

CHOCOLATE WEDGES

Stand these wedges atop a frosted cake or a cream-topped pie to literally add an extra dimension to the dessert.

TOTAL TIME: 15 MINUTES PLUS COOLING
MAKES: 16 WEDGES

½ CUP SEMISWEET CHOCOLATE CHIPS   2 TEASPOONS VEGETABLE SHORTENING

---

1 On 10-inch-long sheet of waxed paper, with toothpick, trace circle using bottom of 9-inch round cake pan; cut out circle. Place cake pan, bottom side up, on surface; moisten slightly with water. Place waxed-paper circle on pan (water will keep paper from sliding).
2 In heavy 1-quart saucepan, combine chocolate chips and shortening. Melt over very low heat, stirring frequently, until smooth.
3 With narrow metal spatula, evenly spread melted chocolate mixture on waxed paper. Refrigerate until chocolate is firm, about 30 minutes.
4 Heat blade of long knife in hot water; wipe dry. Quickly but gently, cut chocolate into wedges. Use wedges to garnish cakes and pies.

CHOCOLATE BUTTERFLIES

Chocolate butterflies are a beautiful and elegant way to dress up chocolate mousse, a frosted cake, or a tart or pie. You can also use the technique to make hearts, flowers, or whimsical shapes of your own design.

TOTAL TIME: 20 MINUTES PLUS COOLING

MAKES: 10 BUTTERFLIES

---

2 SQUARES (2 OUNCES) SEMISWEET
   CHOCOLATE, CHOPPED

1 TEASPOON VEGETABLE SHORTENING

1 Cut waxed paper into ten 4" by 2½" rectangles. Fold each rectangle crosswise in half to form 2" by 2½" rectangle. With pencil, draw outline of half a butterfly on each folded rectangle, using center fold for butterfly body (the pressure of the pencil point will mark the other half of paper as well). Unfold rectangles and place on clean, firm flat surface, tracing side down. Tape rectangles to surface, about 2 inches apart, with small pieces of cellophane or masking tape.

2 In heavy 1-quart saucepan, melt chocolate and shortening over low heat, stirring frequently, until smooth. Remove from heat; cool 10 minutes. Spoon mixture into small pastry bag fitted with small plain tip. Pipe chocolate mixture onto each waxed-paper rectangle in thin continuous line over tracing to make a butterfly. Repeat with remaining chocolate to make 10 butterflies in all.

3 Remove tape. With wide spatula, carefully lift each piece of waxed paper and place, chocolate side up, in 2½-inch muffin-pan cup or in section of empty egg carton so that waxed paper on center fold is slightly bent. Refrigerate until chocolate is set, at least 1 hour. With cool hands, carefully peel off waxed paper. Use butterflies to garnish cakes or pies.

STENCILS

Stenciling is a quick and easy way to decorate an unfrosted cake.

1 Cut lightweight cardboard or manila file folder at least 1 inch larger all around than desired design. With mat knife or single-edge razor blade, cut out stars, triangles, or other shapes of different sizes.

2 Place stencil over unfrosted cake. Sift unsweetened cocoa, confectioners' sugar, or cinnamon sugar over top. Carefully lift off stencil to reveal design. Repeat as desired.

INDEX

Baking dishes, 14
Baking powder, 13
Baking soda, 13
Beating egg whites, 53
Beverages, 159, 160–163
    Coffee-Spiked Hot
        Chocolate, 163
    Frosty Cappuccino, 161
    Hot Chocolate, 160
    Hot Dark Chocolate, 163
    Mexican Hot Chocolate,
        163
    Winter Cocoa Mix, 162
Bittersweet chocolate, 11
Butter vs. margarine, 13

Cakes, 16–61. See also
    Desserts; Frostings
    about: baking tips, 17
    Black-and-White
        Cupcakes, 57
    Black Forest Cake,
        34–35
    Checkerboard Cake,
        28–29
    Chocolate Angel Food
        Cake, 51
    Chocolate Bourbon-
        Pound Cake, 43
    Chocolate Génoise with
        Ganache, 36
    Chocolate Layer Cake,
        16, 18
    Chocolate Nemesis, 37
    Chocolate Pound Cake
        with Irish Whiskey-
        Cream Sauce, 44–45
    Chocolate, Prune, and
        Nut Torte, 42
    Classic Devil's Food
        Cake, 24, 25

Double-Chocolate
    Bundt Cake, 46, 47
Easy Chocolate-
    Buttermilk Cake,
    20–21
Fabulous Flourless
    Chocolate Cake, 38–39
Fallen Chocolate
    Soufflé Roll, 52–53
Flourless Chocolate-
    Hazelnut Cake, 40–41
German's Chocolate
    Cake, 26–27
Milk Chocolate
    Cheesecake, 58–59
Molten Chocolate
    Cakes, 54, 55
Old-Fashioned Cocoa
    Cake, 22
One-Bowl Chocolate
    Cake, 19
Rich Chocolate Cake, 23
Rich Chocolate
    Cupcakes, 56
Sacher Torte, 32–33
Silken Chocolate
    Cheesecake, 61
Triple-Chocolate
    Cheesecake, 60
Triple-Chocolate Cherry
    Cake, 48–49
Triple-Chocolate Fudge
    Cake, 30–31
Warm Chocolate
    Banana Cake, 50
Cheesecakes, 58–61, 101
Chocolate
    basics, 11–12
    history of, 9–10, 162
    making of, 10
    types of, 11
Chopping chocolate, 12

Choux pastry dough, 149
Cocoa, unsweetened, 11
Confections
    Amaretto Truffles,
        118–119
    Chocolate-Dipped
        Dried Fruit, 128–129
    Chocolate Panforte, 115
    Chocolate Truffles, 116
    Chocolate Walnut
        Fudge, 124
    Chunky Black and
        White Chocolate Bark,
        126, 127
    Crackly Chocolate
        Almonds, 123
    Creamy Fudge, 124–125
    Mocha Truffles, 117
    Peanut Butter Cups,
        120–121
    Peanut-Chocolate Balls,
        122
Cookies, 102–129. See also
    Confections
    Amaretto Truffles,
        118–119
    Apricot Fudgies, 110–
        111
    baking tips, 103
    Chocolate Macaroon
        Sandwiches, 105
    Chocolate-Mint
        Sandwiches, 104
    Chocolate Pretzels, 113
    Double-Chocolate
        Biscotti, 112
    Double Chocolate-
        Cherry Drops, 108
    Double-Chocolate
        Chunk Cookies, 109
    Florentines, 102, 114
    Whoopie Pies, 106–107

Cookie sheet tips, 103

Crust. *See* Dough and crust

Decorative pie edge, 83

Desserts. *See also* Frozen desserts
- Amaretto-Chocolate Soufflé, 134–135
- Baked Chocolate-Hazelnut Puddings, 140–141
- Brownie Pudding Cake, 138, 139
- Chocolate Bread Pudding, 143
- Chocolate-Cherry Bread Pudding, 144, 145
- Chocolate Éclairs, 148–149
- Chocolate Fondue with Fruit, 147
- Chocolate Pôts De Crème, 146
- Chocolate Pudding, 136
- Chocolate Soufflés, 132–133
- Chocolate Sticky Toffee Pudding, 142
- Quick Chocolate Pudding Cake, 137

Dough and crust, 77
- about: choux pastry dough, 149; crumb crusts for cheesecakes, 101; decorative pie edge, 83; guidelines, 77
- Chocolate Wafer Crumb Crust, 100
- Graham Cracker Crumb Crust, 100
- Pastry Dough for 1-Crust Pie, 98
- Shortbread Crust, 99
- Vanilla Wafer Crumb Crust, 100

Drinks. *See* Beverages

Dutch-process cocoa, 11

Eggs, 13, 53

Equipment, 14

Extracts, 13

Flour, 13, 45

Fondue, 147

Frostings, 62–75
- about: coloring, 68; figuring quantities, 63
- Chocolate Buttercream Frosting, 63
- Chocolate Glaze, 74
- Cocoa Whipped Cream Frosting, 73
- Coconut-Pecan Frosting, 70
- Coffee Whipped Cream Frosting, 73
- Fluffy White Frosting, 72
- Fudge Frosting, 65
- Ganache, 75
- Intense Chocolate Butter Frosting, 64
- layer cake frosting tips, 27
- Malted-Milk Frosting, 66
- Milk-Chocolate Candy Bar Frosting, 67
- Milk-Chocolate Frosting, 67
- Mocha Glaze, 74
- Peanut Butter Frosting, 71
- Rich Chocolate Frosting, 62
- Semisweet Chocolate Frosting, 66
- Two-Toned Brandied Butter Frosting, 69
- Whipped Cream Frosting, 73
- White Chocolate Buttercream Frosting, 68

Frozen desserts, 150–157
- Brownie Baked Alaska, 156–157
- Brownie Sundae Cups, 152–153
- Chocolate Ice Cream, 150
- Chocolate Sorbet, 151
- Rocky Road Ice Cream Cake, 154–155

Fudge. *See* Confections

Garnishes, 159, 166–170
- Chocolate Butterflies, 169
- Chocolate Curls, 166
- Chocolate Ruffles, 167
- Chocolate Wedges, 168
- Stencils, 170

German's sweet chocolate, 11

Glazes. *See* Frostings

History of chocolate, 9–10, 162

Ice cream. *See* Frozen desserts

Icing. *See* Frostings

Ingredients, 13. *See also specific recipes*

Layer cake frosting tips, 27

Margarine vs. butter, 13
Marshmallow Crème
    Filling, 106
Measuring, 14
Melting chocolate, 12
Meringue, 131
Milk chocolate, 11
Mixers, 14

Nuts, toasting, 93

Pans
    cookie sheet tips, 103
    dusting with flour, 45
    types of, 14
Pastry dough. See Dough
    and crust
Pies and tarts, 76–101
    about: decorative pie
        edge, 83; dough tips,
        77
    Black Bottom Pie, 78
    Brownie Shortbread
        Tart, 96
    Chocolate-Caramel
        Walnut Tart, 94–95
    Chocolate-Cream
        Meringue Pie, 76, 79
    Chocolate Pudding Pie
        with Coconut Crust,
        88
    Chocolate Tartlets, 97
    Chocolate Truffle Tart,
        90–91
    Chocolate Truffle Tart
        with Hazelnut Crust,
        92–93
    Chocolate Wafer Crumb
        Crust, 100
    Chocolate-Walnut Pie,
        85

    Coconut Pastry Crust,
        101
    Dark Chocolate-Walnut
        Caramel Pie, 86, 87
    Favorite Chocolate
        Cream Pie, 80–81
    Fudge Pecan Pie, 82–83
    Georgia Chocolate-
        Pecan Pie, 84
    Graham Cracker Crumb
        Crust, 100
    Pastry Dough for 1-
        Crust Pie, 98
    Shortbread Crust, 99
    Swiss Chocolate
        Almond Tart, 89
    Vanilla Wafer Crumb
        Crust, 100
Puddings, 131. See also
    Desserts

Sauces, 159, 164–165
    Hot Fudge Sauce, 165
    Our Sublime Chocolate
        Sauce, 164
Semisweet chocolate, 11
Sorbet, 151
Soufflés, 131, 132–135
Stencils, 170
Success secrets, 12
Sugar, 13

Tarts. See Pies and tarts
Toasting nuts, 93
Tools, 14. See also Pans
Tortes. See Cakes
Truffles
    Amaretto Truffles,
        118–119
    Chocolate Truffles, 116
    Mocha Truffles, 117

Unsweetened chocolate,
    11
Unsweetened cocoa, 11

White chocolate, 11

PHOTOGRAPHY CREDITS

Sang An: 155

Peter Ardito: 117, 121

Squire Fox: 7

Brian Hagiwara: 8, 35, 111, 165

Lisa Hubbard: 59

iStockphoto: 63, 161; Rafa Irusta Machin: 65; Cathy Britcliffe: 70; Sorin Alexandru: 75

Yunhee Kim: 86

Rita Maas: 6, 39, 125, 153

Steven Mark Needham: 2, 24, 83, 101, 102, 133, 158, 166, 167, 168, 169, 170

Con Poulos: 16

Alan Richardson: 29, 91, 95, 107, 176

Ann Stratton: 49, 76, 81, 119, 126, 129, 138

Mark Thomas: 15, 21, 27, 45, 46, 53, 54, 130, 135, 141, 144, 157

FRONT COVER: Con Poulos
SPINE: Alan Richardson
BACK COVER: Alan Richardson (*top left*); Peter Ardito (*top right*); Mark Thomas (*bottom*)

METRIC EQUIVALENTS CHARTS

The recipes that appear in this cookbook use the standard United States method for measuring liquid and dry or solid ingredients (teaspoons, tablespoons, and cups). The information on this chart is provided to help cooks outside the U.S. successfully use these recipes. All equivalents are approximate.

METRIC EQUIVALENTS FOR DIFFERENT TYPES OF INGREDIENTS

A standard cup measure of a dry or solid ingredient will vary in weight depending on the type of ingredient. A standard cup of liquid is the same volume for any type of liquid. Use the following chart when converting standard cup measures to grams (weight) or milliliters (volume).

Standard Cup	Fine Powder (e.g. flour)	Grain (e.g. rice)	Granular (e.g. sugar)	Liquid Solids (e.g. butter)	Liquid (e.g. milk)
1	140 g	150 g	190 g	200 g	240 ml
¾	105 g	113 g	143 g	150 g	180 ml
⅔	93 g	100 g	125 g	133 g	160 ml
½	70 g	75 g	95 g	100 g	120 ml
⅓	47 g	50 g	63 g	67 g	80 ml
¼	35 g	38 g	48 g	50 g	60 ml
⅛	18 g	19 g	24 g	25 g	30 ml

USEFUL EQUIVALENTS FOR LIQUID INGREDIENTS BY VOLUME

¼ tsp	=					1 ml
½ tsp	=					2 ml
1 tsp	=					5 ml
3 tsp	=	1 tbls	=	½ fl oz	=	15 ml
		2 tbls	= ⅛ cup =	1 fl oz	=	30 ml
		4 tbls	= ¼ cup =	2 fl oz	=	60 ml
		5⅓ tbls	= ⅓ cup =	3 fl oz	=	80 ml
		8 tbls	= ½ cup =	4 fl oz	=	120 ml
		10⅔ tbls	= ⅔ cup =	5 fl oz	=	160 ml
		12 tbls	= ¾ cup =	6 fl oz	=	180 ml
		16 tbls	= 1 cup =	8 fl oz	=	240 ml
		1 pt	= 2 cups =	16 fl oz	=	480 ml
		1 qt	= 4 cups =	32 fl oz	=	960 ml
				33 fl oz	=	1000 ml = 1 L

USEFUL EQUIVALENTS FOR COOKING/OVEN TEMPERATURES

	Fahrenheit	Celsius	Gas Mark
Freeze Water	32° F	0° C	
Room Temperature	68° F	20° C	
Boil Water	212° F	100° C	
Bake	325° F	160° C	3
	350° F	180° C	4
	375° F	190° C	5
	400° F	200° C	6
	425° F	220° C	7
	450° F	230° C	8
Broil			Grill

USEFUL EQUIVALENTS FOR DRY INGREDIENTS BY WEIGHT

(To convert ounces to grams, multiply the number of ounces by 30.)

1 oz	=	¹⁄₁₆ lb	=	30 g
2 oz	=	¼ lb	=	120 g
4 oz	=	½ lb	=	240 g
8 oz	=	¾ lb	=	360 g
16 oz	=	1 lb	=	480 g

USEFUL EQUIVALENTS LENGTH

(To convert inches to centimeters, multiply the number of inches by 2.5.)

1 in =		2.5 cm
6 in – ½ ft =		15 cm
12 in = 1 ft =		30 cm
36 in = 3 ft = 1 yd		= 90 cm
40 in =		100 cm = 1 m

THE GOOD HOUSEKEEPING TRIPLE-TEST PROMISE

At *Good Housekeeping*, we want to make sure that every recipe we print works in any oven, with any brand of ingredient, no matter what. That's why, in our test kitchens at the **Good Housekeeping Research Institute,** we go all out: We test each recipe at least three times—and, often, several more times after that.

When a recipe is first developed, one member of our team prepares the dish and we judge it on these criteria: It must be **delicious, family-friendly, healthy,** and **easy to make.**

1. The recipe is then tested several more times to fine-tune the flavor and ease of preparation, always by the same team member, using the same equipment.

2. Next, another team member follows the recipe as written, **varying the brands of ingredients** and **kinds of equipment.** Even the types of stoves we use are changed.

3. A third team member repeats the whole process **using yet another set of equipment** and **alternative ingredients.**

By the time the recipes appear on these pages, they are guaranteed to work in any kitchen, including yours. WE PROMISE.